THE FIFTH COMMANDMENT

An Era of Patronage

In the Life of

James Augustus Grant

of Viewfield

1810 to 1832

BY

JOHN ROSE-MILLER

2014

Best Wishes

John R M

3

Printed & Published by
For The Right Reasons
60 Grant Street, Inverness IV3 8BS
fortherightreasons@rocketmail.com
Tel: 01463 718844

Reprinted 2014

ISBN: 978-1-910205-00-6

Contents

Illustrations

Introduction

In 1810 James Augustus Grant (JAG) returned to England after a successful fifteen year career in India, described in Volume 1 of his biography.

On learning that two of his brothers had recently died, he felt it his duty to support his aged parents, in keeping with **The fifth Commandment**. It says *"Honour thy father and thy mother that the days of thy life may be long in the land which the Lord thy God giveth thee"*, and is the title of this, the second of three volumes which comprise his biography. It covers the years 1810 to 1832.

JAG's father "Parson John", Minister of Abernethy in Strathspey, died in 1820. His mother died in 1832, the year of the Reform Bill.

JAG purchased the estate of Viewfield in Nairn in 1812. The following spring he married Elizabeth Mackintosh of Millbank. They had a family of one son and seven daughters.

He kept in touch with his former colleagues in India and was able through them to help the careers of several friends and relations. His brother and two of his brothers-in-law left children by Indian ladies. They had contrasting fortunes.

One of the documents contained in JAG's archive is the Roup Roll for the sale at the Manse of Abernethy of the contents of the house together with the crops and livestock on the Minister's glebe, following the death of Parson John in 1820. It lists 784 lots, the purchaser of each and their address plus the amount realised ranging from 1d to £34-10/-. A copy of the Roll, covering twenty six pages, has been printed separately.

He embarked on a second career as a Burgh Councillor, for both Nairn and Forres. He was Provost of the latter for three terms of three years.

Quotations from a number of letters bring to life the people with whom he was associated against the background of the last years of the Napoleonic War and its aftermath. An influencial friend was Colonel Francis Grant who acted as procurator for his "mad" elder brother the 5th Earl of Seafield in a similar way to that in which his contemporary the Prince Regent, the future George IV, acted for his "mad" father King George III.

Radical changes were to take place in 1832. JAG's latter years from then until his death aged ninety one in 1868 are described in a third and final volume entitled "Viewfield", the name by which he became known.

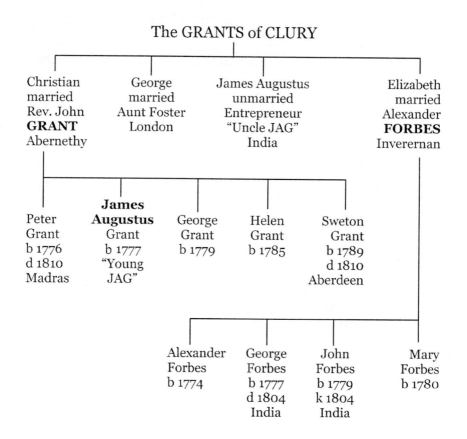

The GRANTS of CLURY

Christian
married
Rev. John
GRANT
Abernethy

George
married
Aunt Foster
London

James Augustus
unmarried
Entrepreneur
"Uncle JAG"
India

Elizabeth
married
Alexander
FORBES
Inverernan

Peter
Grant
b 1776
d 1810
Madras

**James
Augustus**
Grant
b 1777
"Young
JAG"

George
Grant
b 1779

Helen
Grant
b 1785

Sweton
Grant
b 1789
d 1810
Aberdeen

Alexander
Forbes
b 1774

George
Forbes
b 1777
d 1804
India

John
Forbes
b 1779
k 1804
India

Mary
Forbes
b 1780

Figure 1 - Family Tree of the Grants of Clury

Book I – Taking Stock

1. Fifteen Years in India

"The Chairman and Deputy Chairman of the East India Company present their compliments to Mr Grant and request the favor of his company to dine with the Gentlemen of the Direction at the City of London Tavern on Wednesday next the 18th instant at 6 o'clock."

James Augustus Grant received this invitation on the 14th of July 1810, shortly after his return to England after 15 years service in the Company's Bombay Presidency.

Thanks to an introduction from his Uncle and namesake, the first James Augustus Grant, James had been received as a teenager into "the family" of the Governor of Bombay, the Hon Jonathan Duncan. Three years later he was appointed the Governor's Private Secretary. At the age of twenty five, he became the Chief Secretary to the Government of Bombay. As such he had many dealings with the Court of Directors in London.

During this period Marquis Wellesley was Governor General of India. He effected the final downfall of Tippoo Sultan, the Tiger of Mysore, and the subjugation of the predatory Mahrattas. Wellesley annexed to the Company large areas of India, granting subsidiary treaties to local rulers.

Always in his mind was the need to prevent any French incursion into the sub continent, Britain having been at war with republican France since 1793.

In addition to carrying out his routine duties as Chief Secretary to the Government of Bombay, James was heavily involved in administering support for the Governor General's proactive operations. Being very conscientious, his health began to suffer from overwork. Eventually Jonathan Duncan relieved him by nominating him as a Judge in the newly annexed Province of Gujerat north of Bombay. He was both an able administrator and a good Judge.

An account of his childhood in Strathspey and career in India can be found in a companion volume entitled "And a Good Judge Too".

After fifteen years service he had the opportunity of returning home and was awarded an annuity by the Trustees of the Bombay Civil Fund.

It was not every returning civil servant who was invited to dine with the Directors. James was apparently highly thought of, and, had circumstances been different, stood a realistic chance of gaining high office within the Company. Events occurred which dissuaded him from pursuing such a promising career.

James's aged father the Rev John Grant had been Minister of the parish of Abernethy since 1765. He was affectionately known as "Parson John". His wife, Christian, was a Grant of Clury. She had two brothers; James Augustus Grant in India, known as Uncle JAG, the friend of Governor Duncan; and George Grant who lived in London. Uncle George Grant married an heiress, "Aunt Foster". They had an estate in Norfolk and a house at 177 Piccadilly in London.

A family tree (figure 1) sets out some of James's immediate family.

He wasted no time before calling on Uncle George. He was greeted with the melancholy news of the death of his youngest brother Sweton, who had been a divinity student at Aberdeen and was only twenty. His parents had been relying on his support following the marriage of their only daughter Helen to her cousin Alex Grant of Dellachapel. The young couple were now living in Glasgow, two days journey from Abernethy.

Uncle George had written to Parson John commiserating with him and his wife, but cheering them with the prospect of the imminent return home of James and hopefully, in the not too distant future, of their other two sons, Peter and George.

They were to receive a second blow when the news came of the death of their eldest son Peter in Madras just two weeks after James had set sail from Bombay. Knowing him to be ill, James had sent him funds, but had not realised how serious his condition was.

James's younger brother, George Grant, was a Captain in the Company's army, serving in Gujerat. Unknown to his parents, who would not have approved, he had fallen in love with an Indian lady and fathered a child by her. It was not unusual for young men, starved of female company of their own race, to form liaisons with attractive Indian ladies. A prime example was James Kirkpatrick the Resident at the Court of the Nizam of Hyderabad. James knew that his brother was unlikely to abandon the mother of his child and that an addition to the family was on the way. It would therefore fall to him to provide what comfort he could to his afflicted parents. Besides, he yearned to see them again after so long an absence.

James, like his father, had a simple trust in God. As a child he had been brought up to observe the ten commandments. **The 5th Commandment** advised, *"Honour thy father and thy mother that the days of thy life may be long in the land which the Lord Thy God giveth thee"*.

James did not consciously aspire to longevity but did in fact live to be ninety one.

This was an outcome not anticipated by the Trustees of the Bombay Civil Fund who had granted him an annuity of £400 for life, in the belief that members of the Company serving an appreciable time in India had a life expectancy scarcely half of his eventual age. The annuity was payable to his London agents, Porcher & Co.

As a canny Scot, he had saved much of his substantial salary as Chief Secretary to the Government of Bombay and subsequently as senior judge of the Court of Circuit and Appeal in Gujerat. These funds were being transferred from his agents in Bombay, Forbes & Co. The principal partner, Charles Forbes, had put him in the way of adding to his savings by introducing him to a syndicate insuring vessels and their cargoes. All in all, by the time he had received some back pay granted on the recommendation of Governor Duncan, he was reckoned to be worth close to £20,000.

James had spent the four month sea journey home round the Cape in the company of his long time friend and fellow Scot, Alexander Walker. They had first met when James was in Governor Duncan's Secret Intelligence Department and Alex was Military Secretary to General Stuart, the C-in-C of the Bombay Presidency's army. Alex went on to be Military Auditor General at the time when James was Chief Secretary of Bombay. Finally when James was a Judge in Gujerat, Alex was stationed in the adjacent state of Baroda where he was the Resident at the Court of the Guicwar.

On their long journey home, James and Alexander Walker had discussed their future prospects. Hopefully they would each meet a suitable young lady who might be persuaded to marry a middle aged bachelor and settle down on a modest country estate. First of all they would see to their aged parents. Walker's widowed mother was living in Edinburgh and James's parents were at the Manse of Abernethy in Strathspey.

After making certain financial arrangements, and dining with the Gentlemen of the Direction, James set out for the North.

2. State of Affairs in 1810

James's parents were overjoyed to see him again. He had left them as a teenager. In a few days time, on 6th August 1810, he would be thirty three. He was very fit, modestly self-assured and a source of pride to his father and of comfort to his mother. There was much they had to tell each other.

Parson John was still in the habit of keeping his parishioners informed about what was going on in the wide world after delivering his Sunday sermons.

Napoleon had inflicted a crushing defeat on the Austrians. His brother Joseph had been installed in Madrid as King of Spain. Britain's attempt at supporting the Spanish had ended with the retreat of Sir John Moore to Corruna in the north west of the Iberian Peninsular. The only good news was the stout resistance of the Portuguese aided by a British army under General Arthur Wellesley. They had forced Marshal Soult to give up his recent occupation of Oporto and the Douro valley. An attempt had been made to assist the Spanish in reclaiming Madrid. The French had been given a bloody nose at the battle of Talavera. It became evident however that the Spanish, though brave fighters, were no match for the seasoned French Imperial armies. Threatened with encirclement General Wellesley prudently withdrew to Portugal.

Anticipating a concerted effort by the French to overrun the whole peninsula and oust Britain from any foothold on the continent of Europe, he had prepared a strong defensive position at Torres Vedras north of the Portuguese capital of Lisbon. Napoleon ordered Marshal Soult to eliminate any further Spanish resistance and Marshal Massena to clear Portugal of the British.

In May 1810 when James was on the high seas Massena began his invasion of Portugal. Many wondered what chance the "Sepoy General" had of withstanding the all-conquering French armies.

James had on several occasions corresponded with Arthur Wellesley, the younger brother of Marquis Wellesley the Governor General of India. Arthur had been involved in the successful assault on Tippoo Sultan's fortress of Seringapatam in 1799. In 1803, at the battle of Assaye, although heavily outnumbered, he had defeated the Mahrattas, who were supported by the French. James had friends in the Seaforth Highlanders who passed through Bombay before and after the battle. They were in no doubt that Arthur Wellesley was a master of military tactics, decisive and an inspiring leader. Massena could be in for a rude shock.

It subsequently transpired in September that he was halted in his tracks at the battle of Bussaco. Eventually he reached the Lines of Torres Vedras which he was unable to penetrate. Starved of supplies he was forced to withdraw ignominiously from Portugal suffering further defeat at the battle of Fuentes de Onoro. Parson John enthusiastically kept his congregation up to date with events. Though a man of God, he was filled with patriotic feelings. He had been appointed Chaplain to the local Militia which was raised when a French invasion seemed imminent.

The story is told of his announcing the demise of the Emperor Napoleon. When it turned out to be a false rumour he embarrassingly had to admit the following Sunday that what he had announced was untrue and that "that scoundrel" was still alive and causing as much trouble as ever.

He was fascinated to learn from James the background to events in India and the Middle East. At home they had followed Napoleon's invasion of Egypt in 1798 and Nelson's destruction of his fleet at the battle of the Nile. When he returned to France and declared himself First Consul his army attempted to advance to Syria but was thwarted by the gallant defence of the stronghold of Acre led by Sir Sydney Smith. In the nearby seaside town of Nairn they had named one of their streets "Acre Street" in honour of the event.

Later James's brother George Grant and his cousin John Forbes had been part of General Baird's expedition from India sent to drive the French out of Egypt. They had given him a first hand account of it on their return to Bombay.

One of James's assignments, when he was Private Secretary to Governor Duncan, was to establish an overland route for despatches between India and Constantinople where Lord Elgin was Ambassador to the Turkish Court. Contact could then be made with London via Vienna. He travelled through the Persian Gulph, Basra, Bagdad and the old testament lands of Babylon and Ur of the Chaldees.

Parson John was particularly anxious for news of his brother-in-law Uncle JAG.

When James was leaving India his uncle had written from Gorruckpoor in Oude to thank him for his financial support when a Sheriff's officer threatened him with incarceration in a debtors prison. He had made and lost successive fortunes in opium and indigo. Uncle JAG had helped his nephew "Young JAG" at the start of his career. He died in November 1810.

Later, an inscription on the tomb of James Augustus Grant Esqr of Gorruckpoor in the East Indies was written by Mr James Wilkinson, under whose direction the monument was raised. It read as shown opposite.

Sacred to the memory
of
James Augustus Grant Esquire
Who departed this life on the 4th day of November
in the year of our Lord 1810
After a residence in India of twenty eight years
during which period in the pursuit of honorable
independence
through the medium of Commercial Speculation. He
experienced in an uncommon degree
the Vicissitudes of Fortune
retaining however through a long series of unmerited
misfortunes that firmness of mind for which he had
ever been distinguished
He rendered himself no less respected in Adversity
by a cheerful manly & pious resignation
than he was beloved in Prosperity
for his generous and boundless Benevolence
Humane in Disposition
mild and conciliatory in Manners
acute in discerning, sound in judgement
and inflexible in his Integrity
He commanded the general esteem & confidence
of the Natives to whom he was a liberal Patron
a warm friend and a discreet Adviser
and by whom his Memory will long be cherished with
affectionate Veneration
Far from those Relations whose welfare and interests
it had been through life his study to promote and
the sincerity of whose attachment was the
principal solace of his declining years, the
Circle of his Friends at Gorruckpoor to whom he
was endeared by every quality
that can adorn or dignify human nature
seek some alleviation of their sorrow for his life
in paying this last mournful tribute to
departed worth

Owing to a misunderstanding, relations between him and his family in the Highlands had turned sour following the death of his nephew John Forbes, killed at the battle of Dieg in 1804. According to a copy of his will, Uncle JAG had been named as his executor. He had made repeated efforts to obtain the original will, without which he could not act. Eventually he had to take John's fellow officer to court to obtain it. When John's relations heard nothing they drew the conclusion that Uncle JAG had used the proceeds of his nephew's estate to his own ends, being severely embarrassed financially. Parson John's apology for doubting him had been generously accepted.

James took the first opportunity to visit his aunt Betty Forbes at Inverernan in Strathdon to share with her all that he knew of her sons' activities in India. He had sailed to India at the same time as her son George who had stayed initially with Uncle JAG in Benares. After eight years his health deteriorated and James invited him to take a sea journey to join him in Bombay. A few months later he died and James arranged his funeral and saw to his affairs. News of his brother's death reached John Forbes days before he himself died, being killed instantly by a cannon ball after taking an enemy battery in the battle of Dieg. The residue of his estate was left to his sister Mary.

3. Paternal Aunts and their Legacy

James until now had had more to do with his mother's relations than his father's. He was keen to learn more about the latter.

Parson John's only brother, Patrick, had died unmarried in Jamaica in 1802. He had been a planter of sugar cane. His will, or rather the inventory of his estate, had been of some concern to James's father.

The last will of Patrick Grant, Planter, Parish of Kingston, County of Surrey in Jamaica provided for -
1. Payment of just debts and funeral expenses.
2. To each married sister £260.
3. To each unmarried sister £360.
4. To Robert Grant my relation and executor £100.
5. The residue to my brother John Grant Minister of Abernethy.

He nominated as executors -

"My brother John Grant; Donald Davidson, in the parish of Kingston, merchant; William Falconer in the parish of St Catherine Esqr; Robert Grant in the parish of St Ann, planter."

William Falconer arranged for an inventory of the estate and forwarded the proceeds to Parson John.

The inventory read -

	£	s	d
Billy £140, Milton £130, Robert £100,			
Joe £120, Douglas £120, Lucy £120	730.00		00
Due by Donald Davidson including interest	4,773.18		04
Hire of negroes to Alexr McGregor to 21 Jan 1802	68.06		03
Hire of negroes to David Palmer 21 Jan– 15 Mar 1802	18.00		00
A silver watch, gold sleeve buttons and wearing apparel to Mr Robert Grant			

£5,590.04.07

A number of Parson John's relations had emigrated to the West Indies to take advantage of the lucrative trade in sugar. The production of sugar cane was labour intensive and relied on the importation of slaves from West Africa. Their transportation was almost exclusively carried out by English vessels based on Bristol and Liverpool. Since Britain controlled the sea routes across the Atlantic it was difficult for any other nation to participate.

In the late 1700s attempts had been made in parliament to abolish the slave trade. These were opposed by merchants with vested interests. Eventually in 1807 William Wilberforce managed to get a Bill through parliament abolishing the trade. Transportation became illegal and the supply of new slaves to British plantations ceased. However those that were there could not obtain their freedom until the passing of the Reform Bill of 1832

By the time that Parson John received details of his brother's estate the slaves had been sold to other planters and the proceeds forwarded to him. The idea of human beings, however humble, being possessed body and soul by others was anathema to him, but this was a fait accompli. One slave was named Milton, after the family home, Milton of Duthil.

He was obliged as executor to distribute the proceeds amongst his sisters as follows –

Eliza Grant widow of William Grant	£260
Anne Grant married to John Cockburn	£260
Margaret Grant married to John Clark	£260
Mary Grant unmarried at Grange Green	£360
Janet Grant unmarried at Duthil	£360

During the autumn of 1810 James visited four of the Aunts. Aunt Janet had died shortly after receiving her legacy.

A family tree, overleaf, shows James's paternal Cousins, Uncle and five Aunts.

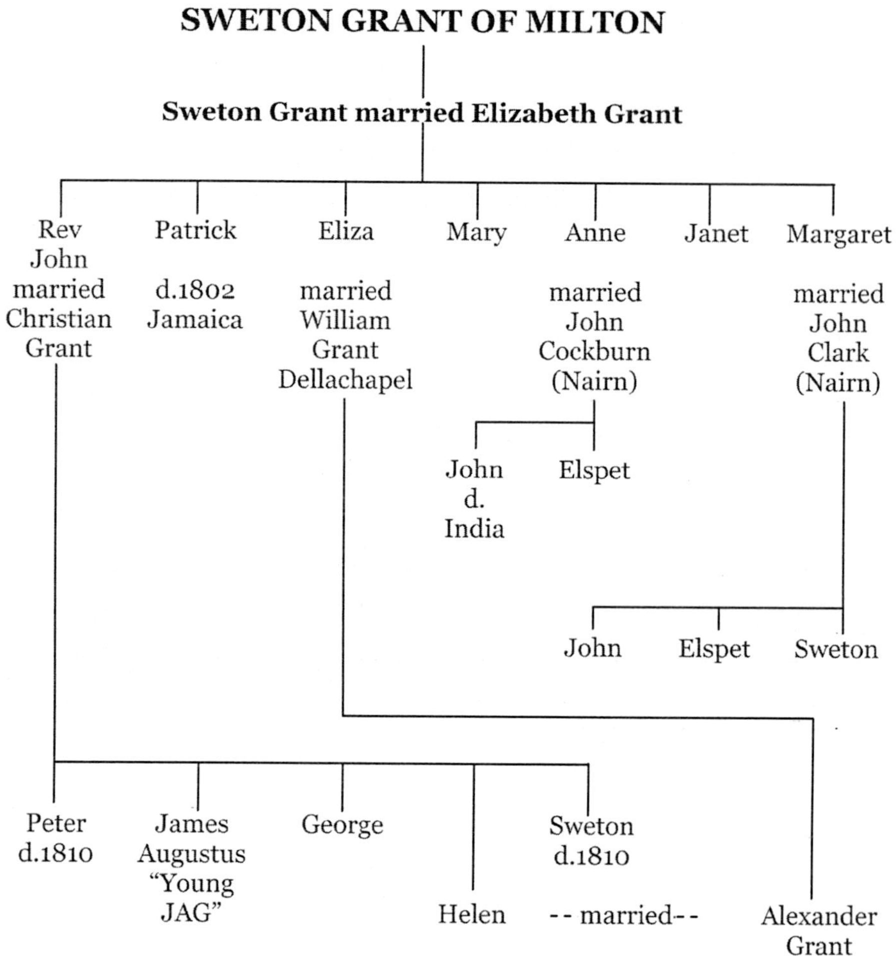

SWETON GRANT OF MILTON

Sweton Grant married Elizabeth Grant

Rev John married Christian Grant	Patrick d.1802 Jamaica	Eliza married William Grant Dellachapel	Mary	Anne married John Cockburn (Nairn)	Janet	Margaret married John Clark (Nairn)

John d. India — Elspet

John — Elspet — Sweton

Peter d.1810	James Augustus "Young JAG"	George		Sweton d.1810	

Helen -- married -- Alexander Grant

Figure 2 - Family Tree of the Grants of Milton

John Cockburn had married Aunt Anne on 18 July 1789 in Nairn where he was a merchant. Their children were born there; John on 18 Sep 1790 and Elspet on 21 Sep 1792. In 1795 John Cockburn was a witness at the baptism in Nairn of his niece Elspet Clark. He was described as factor to the Dalvey Estates near Forres. In 1797 he was a Lieutenant in John Fraser's Company of the Nairnshire Militia Volunteers. James was shown his commission granted to him by George III, King of Great Britain, <u>France</u> and Ireland. Britain had been at war with Republican France since 1793 and evidently the King still laid claim to that country!

There was a short break in the war following the "Peace of Amiens" in 1802. James remembered Governor General Wellesley's refusal to return to the French any of the possessions previously wrested from them, as he was obliged to do under the terms of the Treaty. He correctly anticipated that Napoleon had no intention of keeping to his side of the bargain and that a state of war would soon be resumed. When Napoleon immediately massed his armies for a cross channel invasion of England, many companies of militia were reformed. In 1803 John Cockburn again received a commission, this time as a Lieutenant in the Elgin and Morayshire Corps of Infantry Volunteers.

His son John had applied for a cadetship in the East India Company army. James, through his contacts, arranged for him to get one on the

Bombay establishment. This was the first of many occasions on which James used his connections in the HEIC to get employment for his relations and friends. It was the age of Patronage. Tragically young John Cockburn was to die on board ship the day before it reached Bombay. The news was relayed to James by his friend, and successor as First Secretary, Francis Warden, who had been primed to meet him.

Margaret Clark's husband was a merchant in Nairn. Aunt Margaret and the children had seen James off when he joined the mail coach for Aberdeen, in Nairn, fifteen years ago. Young John Clark also favoured the army and James was to get him the offer of an ensigny in the Regiment (the 66th) of General Nicolls, who had been C-in-C of the Bombay army when James was Chief Secretary. He was not to take up the offer and had a somewhat chequered career thereafter. Elspet never married. Sweton was bound for the sea, sailing as an apprentice on a Glasgow vessel destined for the West Indies in 1815.

James's unmarried Aunt, Mary Grant, rented a house in Nairn near her married sister Mrs Clark. With three of his aunts living in that town, on the coast of the Moray Firth, James naturally paid it frequent visits, especially after he met his future wife there.

Back in 1810 he decided to visit his sister Helen in Glasgow before the onset of winter. At the time they were staying at 94 Hutcheson Street where her husband Alex Grant of Dellachapel carried on a business trading with the West Indies. His family owned the small estate of Dellachapel on the east bank of the Spey below Grantown. The couple were first cousins, Alex's father having married Parson John's sister Eliza. They were to have many children. Their eldest son they called James Augustus. He was the third in a long, often confusing series, of James Augustus Grants. Helen had been only eight when her brother James left for India. Whilst first a bit in awe of him, as he seemed to know so many important people, he soon made her feel more at ease.

Having done the rounds of his relations, he returned home in December via Edinburgh hoping to meet his friend Alexander Walker.

4. Comparing Notes with Alexander Walker

Unfortunately Alex had just left Edinburgh for the Country. James wrote to him from Perth and on reaching home received this reply -

"My dear Grant
I am just returned from my excursion into the Country and have received your letter from Perth. I was particularly disappointed not to see you, being especially anxious for us to meet in the circumstances which the enclosed will explain."

He enclosed a copy of the following letter from the Chairman of the HEIC, William Anstell, and Deputy Chairman, Jacob Bosanquet, who wrote –

"It being in contemplation to make some new appointments to the Bombay Council; and considering as we do, that you from your long residence in Bombay must have acquired a knowledge of the character and abilities of the Civil Servants of that Presidency, we shall esteem ourselves much obliged to you if you will candidly state to us your opinion of the fitness of the under mentioned Persons for the Office in question; and we beg to have it understood that this application to you is not official and that your answers will also be considered as of a very confidential nature. We shall also be much obliged if you will suggest the name of any other Gentleman whom you think we may have omitted & whose abilities may be known to you.

Fredrk Reeves	*George Browne*	*Alexr Bell*
John Smee	*N H Smith*	*P P Travers"*

He also enclosed his reply –

"The Company's Civil Service of Bombay unquestionably contains Gentlemen of real merit, whose names are not comprised in the list of the present candidates. It would be invidious and might appear presumptuous in me to select those Gentlemen for the notice of the Court of Directors; But if I was to give way to my feelings of public duty and private friendship, I would point out Mr James A Grant and Mr Francis Warden, as peculiarly fitted to fill an appointment in the Council of Bombay. These Gentlemen possess a respectability and integrity of Character which, aided by the advantages of Education and experience derived from having ably and honorably filled the first offices under Government, form the most secure basis of qualification for a member of the Company's Councils. It is men of this description who should if possible be selected to fill the appointments to Council, who carry in their own characters the weight and dignity necessary to maintain respect and to uphold the interests of a great Empire.

Among the young Gentlemen who are an honour to the Company's Civil Service I conceive Mr Diggle to stand conspicuous. This Gentleman at an early period was entrusted with important offices in Guzerat, where his conduct was distinguished by temper and moderation, and a regard for Justice, which gained him the confidence of the Natives; and I had frequently the advantage of his assistance. I am of the opinion that the talents of the Gentleman will qualify him for the most honourable situation in their service.

It is no doubt difficult for those who write of their contemporaries, to deliver their sentiments without some bias or partiality - But I can safely say that I am only conscious of affording my opinion for the public honor and advantage and with a full and grateful recollection of the benefits that I have received myself from the Company Service."

Alex added -

"I daresay the enclosed correspondence will have surprised you, but you must not communicate it to any person, as I have yet done to none except yourself. If I had not made so free with your name I should have been silent even to you, or at least have waited until we met, which was indeed one reason of my anxiety to see you. It was a very disagreeable task to reply to the letter from the Chairs. I have however in my reply said nothing to injure any person. I do not imagine your aims at present extend to the honours of Council and what I have said would contribute nothing. At any rate keep the subject secret. Both Rickard and Lachmire are I understand to be removed, but it is not yet settled who are to be their successors. Torin has received permission to return to the service, but under the circumstances of having forfeited the 'confidence of the Court'."

Alex went on to tell of the death of his mother which happened late in December (1810). No symptoms of decay had been discovered so it was most unexpected. She had promised to enjoy life for a series of years. He was now planning a visit to London to pursue his claims against the Company. James's namesake Charles Grant, later to become Lord Glenelg, had promised his support to the full extent of his claims.

On 2 April 1811 Alex wrote –

"After this long silence I am anxious to hear what has become of you and how you intend disposing of yourself during the summer. My time has been a good deal occupied in prosecuting my claims at the India House and now that they are all decided on I shall have little to detain me here. My mind is however at present occupied with my brother's return to India, a measure which has been found prudent if not necessary, but to undertake a second time this distant voyage and to expose himself again to the accidents of war and the climate must excite painful reflections. After his departure I shall not long delay my return to Scotland where I propose to settle myself for life and employ myself in draining, planting and enclosing. To render these rural occupations my dear Grant less solitary I have engaged a partner and if report speaks with truth you are about to contract a similar engagement. The Lady unto whom I am to confide my future destiny is Miss Montgomery - a relation of my own and with whose family a close intimacy has always subsisted. I have now made my confession, tho rather awkwardly.

The appointments to the Council at Bombay would surprise you. I have learnt many curious particulars which I cannot relate, but success was prosecuted through low channels and favoured by accidents. I conceive had you been on the spot and been solicitous that you might have gone out. Rickards was condemned by his own writings and by a kind of automation. The whole of this business cannot fail to excite a considerable sensation at Bombay and I conceive the Court of Directors are not very well satisfied themselves with their own proceedings.

I have put up at our old hotel since my arrival in Town, but I cannot say that this second visit to London has either gratified or satisfied my expectations. The din and confusion is eternal and while one is always in a crowd we look in vain for society. People, I speak of Indians as well as the rest, meet and separate with the same indifference. I see Thriepland pretty often and he partakes of these feelings more than I would have believed, and draws now a much more favourable contrast between India and this Country than he was disposed to entertain on his first arrival. He is a candidate to succeed Sir James, but he seems to entertain little hopes of success, which I regret.

Let me know what you are about in the North? I trust we shall meet somewhere and I shall be most happy to see you at Bowland.

The Government here is contriving new taxes for us which will as usual reach the pockets of the Landed Proprietors with much more certainty than those of the Merchants . Adieu."

James had hinted in confidence to his friend that he had made the acquaintance of a lady who would make an excellent wife. He had not yet had to confess to becoming engaged! Alex continued to assert that James would have been the first choice to fill the vacancy on the Bombay Council had he wished. Thriepland, a fellow Scot, had been Legal

Counsel to the Government of Bombay and "Sir James" Mackintosh the Chief Judge of the Presidency. Alex had acquired the estate of Bowland by the Gala Water in the parish of Stow, south of Edinburgh.

James reported that he, like Alex, had recently been approached by the Chairman of the HEIC, in this case with a request, *"to furnish him, for his private information, with an account of the state of health in which Mr Crowe was at the period when Mr Grant left India"*. Crowe was the Judge and Magistrate of Surat the principal city in Gujerat when James was Judge of the Court of Circuit and Appeal for that Province. He had apparently suffered a nervous breakdown but by all accounts was back to his normal self.

Surat was in the south of the Province nearest to Bombay. The second most important city in the Province was Broach, centrally situated, where James had resided with his fellow Judges of the Court. The Collector of Broach, who both assessed and "collected" the land tax, William Steadman, had been closely associated with James throughout his stay in Gujerat. He had asked James to acquire for him a pair of guns from the celebrated firm of Mantons in London. They were ordered and despatched by Capt J Michie, a friend of the family, closely associated with the firm of Forbes & Co, on whose vessel the "Cumbria" they were to be sent to Bombay.

After accounting for Steadman's guns Michie wrote

"You will I dare say have been surprised on hearing that George Brown & Elphinstone were appointed to the Council to supercede Lechmire and Rickards, but such is the case. The reason is supposed to be Rickard's systematic opposition to the Governor together with the business of the hemp on the Cumbria. Interest is everything in Leadenhall Street (the Headquarters of the HEIC). *Why did you not exert your interest on this occasion? Reeves I hear feels very hurt as he thought himself sure of a seat in Council and so does that great Nabob Torin..."*

Although James took a keen interest in developments in India and the fortunes of his friends and former colleagues there, it was a world apart from Strathspey and the Highlands where he was enjoying his parents company, renewing old acquaintances and making new ones. One friend in particular was to feature prominently in his future career, Colonel the Honourable Francis Grant of Grant, the youngest son of the Clan Chief.

5. The Seafield – Grant Connection

Clan Grant had for generations occupied the broad lands of Strathspey to the north of the Cairngorms. As time went by others infiltrated the area, but still in James's day every second person was said to be a Grant and many of them were called James. He had in his childhood been embarrassed at having the middle name Augustus, but it had helped to distinguish him from his other namesakes. Now that he had reached a respectable middle age, his full name of James Augustus Grant suited him, lending him a certain air of quiet distinction.

The Chief of the Clan, the feudal superior of most of the land in Strathspey, was also called James. He was justly referred to as "The Good Sir James". His family seat was at Castle Grant eight miles from Abernethy on the opposite side of the Spey. Between the castle and the river, Sir James had laid out the New Town of Grantown with the aim of providing alternative employment to people eking out a precarious living from subsistence farming.

He was a personal friend of Parson John and their families were well known to each other.

Sir James's eldest son, Lewis Grant of Grant, had been a successful lawyer in Edinburgh and an MP. He had been obliged to give up both careers when he developed a brain disorder. Though otherwise healthy, he was incapable of looking after his own affairs. His father acted as his "procurator" with power of attorney. When it became evident that Lewis was not going to recover his faculties, Sir James sought to hand over responsibility for him to his next son James Thomas.

James Thomas Grant of Grant was two years older than James Augustus, and had preceded him to India where he also entered the Company's service as a Writer. For some years he lived in Benares in the Ganges valley close to the home of "Uncle JAG". He became Chief Magistrate of the city. He often corresponded with "Young JAG" 800 miles away in Bombay. James regularly forwarded letters between him and his father. Enclosing one of these James Thomas wrote on the 9 Apr 1802 –

> *"I will be much obliged to you to send the enclosed home by the first despatch over land. This will necessarily be nearly the last time in which I have it in my power to trouble you, at least for some time. It is to inform our friends at home that in 1803 I mean to obey my father's repeated representations to return to Europe. I suppose I'll be two or three years in Britain - if during that time I can be of any use to you, I trust you will not hesitate to call for my services Adieu!"*

In the event he never did make it home, putting off doing so until finally contracting a virulent fever from which he died. It transpired that he had a liaison with an Indian lady by whom he had two children, a fact which explained his reluctance to return home. James had to convey the melancholy tidings to Sir James.

The third of his sons to reach maturity was Francis, the same age as James. He was a colonel in the militia and was known as Col the Hon Francis Grant of Grant. He took over the office of Lewis's procurator from the ageing Sir James.

Not long after James returned from his trip to Glasgow and Edinburgh Sir James died, in Feb 1811. Colonel Francis wrote to James and his close friends from Castle Grant on 25 Feb –

> *"My dearly beloved and most affectionate Father Sir James Grant of Grant Baronet departed this life on Monday evening the 18th Inst. His remains are to be interred upon Thursday first the 28th. Your presence here by 10 o'clock forenoon of that day to accompany his funeral from hence to the Church yard of Duthil, the Family burying place, is requested."*

James sent news of his Chief's death and an account of the funeral to his uncle George Grant in London. At the same time he asked for his advice on investing his funds and acquiring an estate. Uncle George replied –

> *"My dear Nephew*
> *I have been duly favored with your kind letters from Edinburgh and Abernethy. You have been better than good in writing a second letter without receiving a reply to the first. I am well acquainted with the*

benevolence of your disposition which would rather forgive a fault than foment a neglect or misunderstanding never intended, altho with some under the circumstances of much less consideration than your conduct merits, an unpardonable offence would have been heaped on my head. Thank God I have to do with a liberal mind and different character. I am happy to hear your Father and Mother continue to enjoy pretty good health. They have you in a great degree to thank for it, for passing the winter in the North, as your presence in the midst of their affliction, must have relieved them (after so long an absence) very much indeed. I shall be most happy to learn that your own health is on the mending order, but cannot help observing the sudden change of climate was more than prudence could warrant. However as the weather is now fine and you have youth on your side I have no fears of you being soon quite well.

I trust I need not tell you that my family at all times when it suits your convenience will be most happy to have you amongst them and you would be pleased to see Foster (his son) going on with improvements in agriculture on the low ground of the estate producing where let double the rent paid by Mr Gardner. I have let the Upper Farm 510 acres for £1020 a year which does not include any part of the lawn and I have reason to expect the remainder of the Property supposing all let would nearly realize £4000 a year. Foster let several marshes the other day at £4.10.00 per acre, to tenants in the county holding under neighbouring proprietors large arable farms, without grazing land. Notwithstanding of all this I am still kept very much here, winding up stubborn outstanding concerns and denied those comforts which I ought to enjoy with my family.

In my opinion purchasing an estate at the present rate given for land, is the sure way of making an independent man very soon otherwise. It is deemed a good purchase that realizes a net 3%. What a fortune must be invested to make a tolerable income. In short it will not answer to invest in land a moderate fortune as it would prevent the Proprietor from keeping pace with the times, by occasionally laying out his money to a greater legal advantage than 5%, which frequently occurs here.

I am not sorry that you are no longer involved with Clury (the family estate) *as it will give us a chance of seeing you in England. I think I hear your Mother exclaim, how unreasonable in George to try to seduce you from Scotland.*

I had heard of our worthy Chief's death before the receipt of your last letter; there never lived a more honorable or sincere friend than he was, and it will be truly fortunate for Strathspey if his successors prove equally kind and generous. I understand Colonel Francis Grant would have been married before this time had not his worthy Father died. The young Lady has not much Fortune, is of small stature, pleasant manners etc; and he met with her on a visit at Capt Francis Grants, a relation and late Commander of an East India ship which I think he lost going to China.

Foster stands well for the Dalton Estates, whether Mrs Grant (his wife, formerly Miss Dalton) *survives her Parents or not, as it turns out on investigation she possesses the ultimate Fee of the property.* (At that time a husband was entitled to his wife's fortune unless special arrangements were made, which apparently Foster had not agreed to) *...In a few days,* *the beginning of next Term, Foster becomes possessed of a very large Fortune in reversion that noone can prevent him from having. Mrs Foster Grant is quite well and corresponds weekly often with her parents and so did he until he refused to make himself Tenant for life of the Estates, which for the moment has mortified and disappointed his new Papas expectations, altho he offered him for doing so an immediate income but not by £100,000 adequate to the sacrifice he required of him to make. Mrs F G is not yet with child which makes her Parents and Foster view the Free of the Estate as a matter of more consequence, whether they remain with Daltons or become Fosters.*

You will be tired of reading this scrawl. Remember me with affection to your Father and Mother and believe me etc."

Uncle George's advice seemed to be, to follow his own and his son's example and marry a rich heiress, and to avoid tying up all his capital in land.

Another event, which was to influence James's ideas on investing his fortune, was the death of the 4th Earl of Seafield, in October 1811. Sir Lewis Grant, already Chief of the Clan following his father's death in February, succeeded him as the 5th Earl of Seafield. Colonel Francis Grant, as his brother's procurator, became responsible for both the Grant estates and the more extensive Seafield estates.

FINDLATER, SEAFIELD and GRANT Lines of Succession

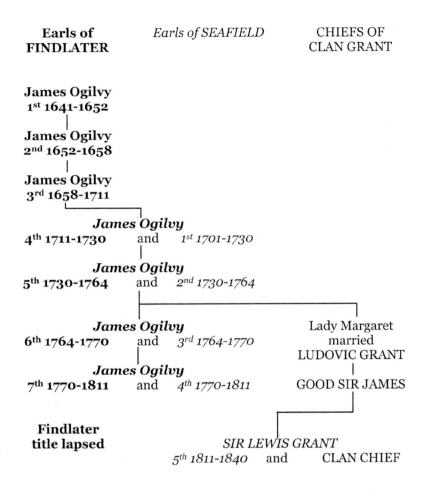

Earls of **FINDLATER**	*Earls of SEAFIELD*	CHIEFS OF CLAN GRANT
James Ogilvy **1st 1641-1652**		
James Ogilvy **2nd 1652-1658**		
James Ogilvy **3rd 1658-1711**		
James Ogilvy **4th 1711-1730** and	*1st 1701-1730*	
James Ogilvy **5th 1730-1764** and	*2nd 1730-1764*	
James Ogilvy **6th 1764-1770** and	*3rd 1764-1770*	Lady Margaret married LUDOVIC GRANT
James Ogilvy **7th 1770-1811** and	*4th 1770-1811*	GOOD SIR JAMES
Findlater **title lapsed**	*SIR LEWIS GRANT* *5th 1811-1840* and	CLAN CHIEF

Figure 3 - The Seafield-Grant Connection

Before the accession of Sir Lewis Grant, the Earls of Seafield (and Findlater) had all been Ogilvies. In 1641 James Ogilvy was created 1st Earl of Findlater. In 1707 the 3rd Earl was one of the signatories of the Treaty of Union, as was his son, who had been created the 1st Earl of Seafield on his appointment as Lord Chancellor of Scotland. When the latter succeeded his father in 1711 he became both the 4th Earl of Findlater and 1st Earl of Seafield. His son held the titles of 5th Earl of Findlater and 2nd Earl of Seafield from 1730 to 1764 and had a son James and daughter Margaret.

Lady Margaret Ogilvy married Sir Ludovic Grant, Chief of Clan Grant. Their only son was the "Good Sir James". Lady Margaret's nephew James Ogilvy, the 7th Earl of Findlater and 4th Earl of Seafield died in October 1811 without issue. The Findlater title lapsed. Provision had been made on the creation of the Seafield title for it to be passed down the female line if there were no male heirs. Lady Margaret's grandson Sir Lewis Grant of Grant therefore became the 5th Earl of Seafield and inherited the Seafield estates.

Colonel Francis's situation, as his brother's procurator, was similar to that of his contemporary the Prince Regent, who acted on behalf of his father, the "mad" King George III. Following the latter's death, in 1820, the Prince Regent became George IV.

Colonel Francis and his young bride made their home at Cullen House in Banffshire. James Augustus visited them often and was well placed to learn of any estates which might come on the market.

On the outskirts of the town of Nairn, situated on the coast of the Moray Firth sixteen miles east of Inverness, the 7th Lord Findlater and other landowners entered into an excambion in 1790, exchanging numerous interspersed "rigs" for a few blocks of land. One block of Findlater land running from the town westward towards the sea was divided into two parallel estates called Seabank and Viewfield. Substantial "Mansions" were built on both estates. The one on Viewfield was built by Colonel Ludovic Grant of Dalvey in 1803 and sold to a Captain Williamson in 1807. The one on Seabank was occupied by William Grant JP. There were rumours that Captain Williamson was thinking of moving to Edinburgh.

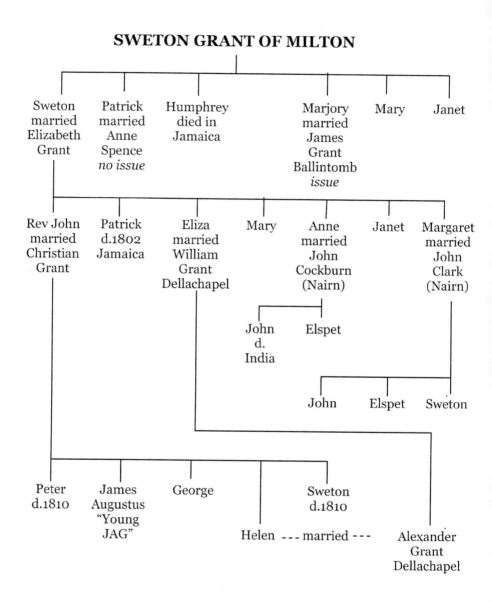

SWETON GRANT OF MILTON

Sweton married Elizabeth Grant	Patrick married Anne Spence *no issue*	Humphrey died in Jamaica		Marjory married James Grant Ballintomb *issue*	Mary	Janet

Rev John married Christian Grant	Patrick d.1802 Jamaica	Eliza married William Grant Dellachapel	Mary	Anne married John Cockburn (Nairn)	Janet	Margaret married John Clark (Nairn)

John d. India — Elspet

John — Elspet — Sweton

Peter d.1810

James Augustus "Young JAG"

George

Sweton d.1810

Helen - - - married - - - Alexander Grant Dellachapel

Figure 4 – Descendants of Sweton Grant of Milton

46

6. Great Uncle Patrick, Calder Minister 1746

James stayed with his parents at Abernethy, during the winter of 1811/12. In the northern latitudes in which Abernethy is situated, the almost perpetual daylight of the summer gave way to the long dark evenings of winter. He spent much of his time browsing, by candlelight, through the collection of books in his father's library. Many of them had been bequeathed to Parson John by his Uncle Patrick, the great uncle of "Young JAG".

The Rev Patrick Grant was Minister of Calder parish at the time of Culloden in 1746. The battle took place in the neighbouring parishes of Croy and Petty on the 16th of April. The local population was almost entirely Presbyterian and had little sympathy for the Catholic Prince Charles and his "rebels". Much of the countryside was ravaged by the opposing armies. Three years after the battle the Rev Patrick was transferred to the parish of Urray in Rossshire. He had a distinguished career. In 1774 he was made a Doctor of Divinity at Kings College, Aberdeen, and was elected Moderator of the General Assembly of the Church of Scotland on 21st May 1778. He died on 14th April 1787.

James was intrigued by his will in which Parson John featured prominently. It nominated no less than eleven persons as his executors, two of whom if they accepted the office would be sufficient to form a quorum. The persons listed were –

"Sir James Grant of Grant Bart my Chief
The Hon Henry Erskine Esq Advocate
The Rev Dr Harry Spence of Kirkton my bro in law
Sir Hector Mackenzie of Gerloch Bart
William Grant of Dellachapple
Dr Gregory Grant Physician Edinburgh
George Gillanders of Highfield
The Rev Colin Mackenzie Minr of Fodderty
Mr George Balfour Minr of Tarbat
Mr Daniel Rose Minr of Dingwall
Colquhoun Grant Clerk to the Signet"

The will stipulated –

"Everything to be sold, except furniture for his well beloved spouse Anne Spence. Proceeds to be used to:

1. Pay just debts & admin expenses
2. Pay yearly to Mrs Anne Spence one thousand merks scots incl an annuity of £20 per our marriage contract + furniture
3. Pay the interest on the remainder to my elder bro Sweton Grant of Miltown or failing him to his spouse Mrs Elizabeth Grant.
4. My Library to go to my nephew Mr John Grant Minister of Abernethy except any books desired by my wife.
5. After the death of my spouse, my bro Sweton & his wife,
  (i) £700 to Rev John Grant Abernethy for use of himself his wife and children.
  (ii) £100 to Patrick, Sweton Grant's eldest son, now in the Island of Jamaica, if he should return.
  (iii) £150 each to my nieces Janet Grant, Anne Grant and Margaret Grant, daughters of Sweton Grant of

48

Milntown. If any of my nieces do not survive me, their share to be divided between her sisters.

(iv) £50 to Patrick Grant third son of Wm Grant Dellachapple by my niece another daughter of Sweton Grant of Miltown.

(v) From the residue make provision for annuities of £3 each for my nieces Janet Grant, Anne Grant & Margaret Grant.

(vi) The balance to be distributed to such of my nieces and nephews as would appear most in need upon their applying to my executors.

I have omitted

(a) The children of my very dear sister Marjory Grant spouse to James Grant late of Ballintomb.

(b) My sisters Mary and Janet.

(c) The children of my natural bro Mr Patrick Grant sometime Minr of Loggie East in Rossshire.

Since they have been sufficiently provided for in the will of my brother Humphrey Grant who died some years ago in Jamaica.

also

(d) My dear wife's relations, since none of them stand in need of my bounty."

Anne Spence died at Forres on 9th September 1793. She and Patrick had been married in Calder on 10th March 1738 but had no children.

The present incumbent of Great Uncle Patrick's former parish of Calder was the Rev Alexander Grant, who had been licenced by the Presbytery of Abernethy. James had met him when he compared notes with Parson John for the statistical accounts of their respective parishes in 1791 and had an open invitation to visit him. In the spring of 1812 he spent a few days at the Manse of Cawdor. He asked why the parish was now called Cawdor instead of Calder.

It was explained that the Laird John Campbell, when created a baron in 1796, had chosen the title Baron Cawdor of Castlemartin, a village in West Wales near the family seat. For many generations the Lairds, as a result of marrying Welsh heiresses, had lived in that country, employing factors to run their Scottish estates. On a visit in 1807 the Laird had made it known that he wished the name to be spelled Cawdor instead of Calder.

James was shown the Session Minutes where the newly appointed Clerk and Schoolmaster (whose salary was paid by the Laird) first entered the name Cawdor. This had been heavily scored out and overwritten Calder. Such was the influence of Lord Cawdor, that inevitably the new name was reluctantly adopted. Shakespeare had called Macbeth Thane of Cawdor in "the Scottish Play". Although it was a name invented by the bard, it was assumed to be the proper spelling by the educated classes. The Rev Grant suggested that the Campbell Lairds did not wish to be reminded every time they visited that they were considered to have usurped the Castle and Estate from the Calder family.

Many generations earlier, the Campbells had become Lairds when the Calder heiress was carried off to Argyll and married to the Earl of Argyll's younger son, Sir John Campbell.

Other pages of the Session Minutes made interesting reading.

At the time of Culloden no mention was made of the nearby battle. However, beforehand, on the 12th of March –

> *"The Minister having got 9 shillings sterling from Gentlemen of the parish for ye benefit of ye Parishioners taken by the highlanders added 11 shillings from the (Poor) Box and sent 20 shillings to Mr Shaw, Minr of Pettie to be given for ye said purpose".*

At the same time

> *"2 shillings was given to Janet Rose, Henwife".*

On the following Sundays, March 16th, 23rd, 30th and April 6th the Lectures in the forenoon were based on 2nd Corinthians and the Texts in the afternoon were from Luke Chapter 2.

There was no service on Sunday the 13th April. The battle took place on Wednesday the 16th. On the following Sunday, the 20th, the Lecture was based on Psalms 124 and 125 and there was no afternoon Sermon. Next Tuesday the 22nd April -

"Mary Munro and David Dennoon acknowledged guilt of uncleanness and cautioners were given for their fines".

The usual services were resumed until the Minister went to attend the General Assembly in Edinburgh in June. On 22nd June -

"An Act of the Assembly for observing a day of Publick Thanksgiving throughout the Nation on ye account of the Late Deliverance from ye Rebellion was read and appointed to be keept thirsday next".

After the sermon on Sunday 29th June –

"Mary Munro was delated (accused) *as guilty of fornication with David Denoon and ordered to be summoned against next Sabbath".*

Things were back to normal.

James noted that in November 1752 the Julian calendar was replaced by the Gregorian. Eleven days had to be added to the old date to give the "New Style" date. The old style Sunday 8th November became the new style 19th. There was unrest amongst the people who demanded that they be given back their eleven days. Had the Gregorian calendar been introduced before the battle of Culloden in 1746, it would have taken place on the 27th April instead of the 16th. Its anniversary would have been on the 27th April in 1812 exactly 66 years later. The hours of daylight and climatic conditions would have differed accordingly. James and the Minister spent some time calculating the repercussions before agreeing to be grateful that whatever the date they were fortunate to be living in a more peaceful Scotland.

Two of the Minister's children still lived in the locality. His daughter Grace was married to Captain William Fraser of Brackla, a village between Cawdor and Nairn. The Captain had just built a whiskey distillery which was to be supplied after the next harvest with barley from the fertile lands bordering the river Nairn. James was given a personal conducted tour.

The Minister's son James Grant, known well into middle age as "Young Jamie" had been a contemporary of James Augustus's young brother Sweton at Kings College Aberdeen. He followed his father into the Ministry and was to become a neighbour and close friend.

James found Nairnshire a friendly place where he would be content to settle if the opportunity arose. Before leaving the Manse of Cawdor he discovered that his host had met a fellow Minister at a recent Assembly called the Rev Shank. His parish was at Laurencekirk and James had visited him on his way back from Edinburgh some months before. His son Henry Shank had been a close friend of his in India and was Political Secretary to the

Government of Bombay when James was Chief Secretary.

On his return to Abernethy a letter awaited him from Henry –

> *"My dear Friend*
> *Your very acceptable letter of December last[1] from Glasgow is before me, for which my best acknowledgements are returned. I am concerned to observe that your health was not altogether as you could have wished, but long before this period I have not the smallest doubt of your being in every respect recovered from the effects of this country & that you are again equal to looking at & deciding upon, a determination in regard to this Country.*
>
> *I mentioned in my last the state of Mr Duncan's health, for which you will not now be surprised when I add that we are told he is just alive & that is all! Poor unhappy man he has been in this state for the last six days and is seen by noone except Forbes[2] and Keir[3]. I have not been with him for three weeks, for his temper latterly has been so bad, that we have all fallen in some measure under his displeasure, and rather than distress him in what I fear are his few remaining days I have merely sent to say that I am ready to attend him the moment I am wanted. In this sad state they talk of putting him on board the Carmarthen for Bourbon, which by many is thought folly & cruelty, and our friend Keir an hour ago told me he thought it of very little consequence what was*

---

[1] 1810
[2] Charles Forbes
[3] Doctor Keir

done as he seemed to think him past all hope of recovery. In the event of his death Brown will succeed as a matter of course until we hear from home, & if he is sufficiently well to go on board the Carmarthen, Genl Abercromby is to be left in charge of the Government.

I am truly happy to learn that you had kindly visited my dear Parents at Laurencekirk; I had due tidings of you before the receipt of your letter, & you may easily believe they were all much delighted & satisfied in meeting so near a friend of mine.

On the 21st ultimo my better half presented me with a son, Alexander the Little, and this far, thank God, Sandy and his Mother are doing as well as I could wish them.

We are told here that if you are inclined to return, a seat at the Board will certainly be in your option, and if you determine to remain, our friend Warden will be the next; in either event I shall be very happy, & since a change I imagine must take place in the Government in the course of a few weeks, or possibly days, one or other will no doubt be the case. Our friend White even begins to look towards the Board & the other day he did not half relish my telling him that I expected to leave Bbay under a salute of 17 guns.

L's business has been determined on by a great majority of the Service & the annuity to which he would have been entitled has been tendered to the next in succession, Gillis I think, but he will not accept it, & then that little Bod Wren will come in. The two annuities in circulation by the return of Brown, & Torin expected on the Scaleby, will go to Lechmire &

Rickards. The latter we are told intends to make a sad stir at the India Ho, on the subject of his removal, & his friends here seemed inclined to think that he has materials & a cause to bring him back as Governor! You will be able to judge of this, but with the present Direction I should think it very improbable. Lechmire too says that he will play the d - l himself with the Chair, Deputy & 24! that he will make them swallow their hostile Paragraphs, & tell them that they are all scamps into the bargain.

My health thank Heaven holds out extremely well, & if the Hble Gents allow me to sit quietly here for four or five years to come, I do not despair of "Knocking down the Petericks" in your Turnip Fields in 1817 or 18 at farthest.

Henry's letter had been written on the 2nd August 1811 but did not reach Abernethy until the following February 1812. It was closely followed by another written on 13th August announcing Jonathan Duncan's death on the 11th. Having served the Governor for so many years, James was saddened to hear of the decline and death of a man for whom he had the greatest respect and affection.

7. Purchase of Viewfield, and Marriage

Letters continued to arrive from his friends and former colleagues in India giving their versions of events. Dr Wallace, surgeon to the Court in Gujerat, wrote of the fever that had swept the Province carrying off, amongst others, Diggle, whom Alexander Walker had recommended to the Chairmen, and the Doctor's own son.

All these events had occurred many months ago and it would be nearly a year before James's reactions to them would reach his correspondents. It was not possible to use the "Overland Route" which he had pioneered because Napoleon was in control of Vienna and much of the continent of Europe. The Emperor was making preparations for his invasion of Russia which was to end so disastrously with his winter retreat from Moscow. The journey round the Cape still had to be conducted in time consuming convoy because of the activities of American privateers. As will be explained later, to effect the blockade of European ports, Britain had intercepted American ships. A period of inept negotiation had culminated in war with the fledgling United States in 1812, and a collapse in trade.

James was still interested in the progress of the war and Indian matters, but was more concerned with developments closer to home.

Alexander Walker had "become a Benedict" with his marriage to Miss Montgomerie. He had made several improvements to his house at Bowland and almost considered himself a farmer. Mrs Walker had given birth to a son who was the centre of attraction. He and his wife constantly looked forward to James visiting them, which he had not yet been able to do. Walker mentioned a number of properties about Edinburgh which could have suited him. There was also the estate of Castlehill near Inverness which had recently come on the market. It would not be in such easy reach however of Abernethy, as would a property in Nairnshire.

Colonel Francis's young wife had introduced him to the pleasures of the dance. As a skilled rider he enjoyed blending his movements to the rhythm of the music. Although a newcomer to this form of entertainment he soon learned the intricacies of the fashionable dances. He did not disgrace himself when standing up with the attractive Miss Mackintosh at the Nairnshire Balls. She was very distantly related to him through the Grants of Knockando, and had been introduced to him by his Aunt Anne Cockburn.

The situation was not unlike that described in Jane Austen's recently published novel "Pride and Prejudice". Its opening line read –

"It is a truth universally acknowledged, that a single man in possession of a good fortune must be in want of a wife".

Fortunately the rumours, that Captain Williamson was planning to leave Nairn for Edinburgh, were true and he readily agreed to sell his estate of Viewfield to James. Elizabeth Mackintosh confided that she would be happy to share her life with him there.

James was grateful for her acquiescence. He did not take it for granted that she would accept his proposal. He was too modest and she had many admirers. He had met her on a number of occasions in the last few months and she had always been friendly and interested in what he had to say. They were in fact well suited, spurning frivolity but not so serious as to miss the humour of situations. James found her to be practical and possessed of an intellect equal to his own. He really was a lucky man and told Alexander Walker so.

The advertisement for the sale of Viewfield in 1807, when it was sold to Captain Williamson, had read –

"TO BE SOLD"

By public roup within the house of George Richardson, innkeeper in Nairn, upon Friday the 18th day of December next, if not previously disposed of by private bargain, THE LANDS, MANSION-HOUSE, OFFICES and GARDEN of VIEWFIELD, with certain other Lands, Half of a Miln, and Half of a Salmon Fishing, & other subjects formerly advertised, situated in the town and close neighbourhood of Nairn. The House of Viewfield is modern, and commodious, and the field in its vicinity substantially inclosed with a stone dyke, and surrounded by a belting of thriving young timber. The Offices are large and substantial, and the Garden measuring upwards of a Scots acre, is inclosed with a stone wall, partly fifteen feet high, the other Lands and Subjects in Nairn, are of considerable yearly value. So neat and compact a property is seldom to be met with in the North, and as the Proprietor is determined to sell far below the real value, a great bargain may be expected. The purchaser may have the elegant Furniture at Viewfield at a fair valuation, and payment of the price will be made convenient to him.

For particulars application may be made to Alexander Grant, Esq W.S. Edinburgh; Alexander Carmichael, Esq, Forres; and Mr Alexander Hay, Sheriff Clerk of Nairn, who is possessed of the title deeds, and will show the premises to intending purchasers."

An early photograph of the Mansion.

Figure 5 - Viewfield

The estate of Viewfield, where they would live, when married, extended to nearly 40 acres on the western outskirts of the town of Nairn. Two thirds was farm land, recently enclosed, while the remaining one third nearest the town contained the Georgian mansion house, offices and an entrance lodge. An avenue of young trees led up to the house.

Parallel to the Viewfield estate on its northern side was the Glebe of the parish church with its manse on the High Street near the Town House.

To the south was the estate of Seabank which like Viewfield had been formed out of the property owned by the 7th Earl of Findlater and 4th of Seafield. It stretched from the High Street westwards to the sea. Set back from the High Street was the mansion of Seabank, home to William Grant a prominent citizen and JP.

On the opposite side of the High Street southwards along the Cawdor Road was a third estate, formed at the time of the 1790 excambion, called Millbank. The farmland was laid out on a plateau above the River Nairn with a mansion at the end nearest the town, where Elizabeth's father Colonel William Mackintosh resided.

Colonel William was the younger brother of Lachlan Mackintosh of Balnespick, whose wife was the sister of Sir Aeneas Mackintosh of Mackintosh.

The Mackintosh, as the chief of the clan was called, lived at Moyhall, to the south, beyond the Nairnshire hills.

The Colonel had visited his friend Ludovick Grant of Knockando when on furlough after serving in the West Indies. There he met his future wife Elizabeth Claudia Guyon, the sister of Ludovick's wife Ann. Soon after they were married, the Colonel was recalled to his regiment which took part in the defence of Gibraltar against the Spanish, one of the last actions of the extended war of American Independence.

Their son William was born at the home of Mrs Mackintosh's other sister Mrs Peter Blaguire in Hampstead. Two more sons, Beauchamp and Guyon were born in Forres and Elizabeth and her younger sister Margaret Mary at Newton in Aberdeenshire. The family moved to Nairn in 1800 when the Colonel bought the estate of Millbank.

In 1812 Elizabeth and Margaret were still at home. William and his wife Jane Galloway had rented Meikle Kildrummie on the Kilravock estate three miles south of Nairn. Beauchamp was a Lieutenant in the HEIC's army in Madras and Guyon was 4th mate on an Indiaman sailing to China.

Elizabeth had come to know the Williamsons and their house when they had taken up residence at

Viewfield five years earlier. It had been newly furnished and it was agreed that James should buy the existing furniture and the stock. He received a receipt from David Williamson on 22 Dec 1812 -

Received this day from James Augustus Grant Esq bill of exchange on Messrs Porcher & Co Devonshire Square London for £417.11.6 payable on 22Mar 1813 in full discharge of balance due to me as per annexed memorandum –

Stocking at Viewfield, per schedule		*£284. 7. 6*
Household furniture per further		
* schedule*		*£268.14. 7*
Melioration on House in "Fishing"		
* Town*		*£1.17.10*
Half of appraiser's bill		*£1.11. 6*
		£556.11. 5
Deduct		
Received on account	*£100*	
Pd by JAG to Mr Fraser		
* my half share of stamp*	*£38*	
Share of chaise to		
* Inverness, expenses etc*	*£6*	
		£144. 0. 0
Balance		*£412.11. 5*
Plus interest for 3 months say		*£5.00. 1*
		£417.11. 6

James asked Porchers to sell sufficient of his 3% Consols to provide for bills of £5,000 payable in March and £3,000 on 1st June 1813. Entry was granted on 22 Dec 1812. (Williamson was due to repay a loan secured on the property before the following June).

When told of the details Alexander Walker wrote -

"I had long been looking out for the intelligence that you had made a purchase and I am happy that you have actually accomplished the object. I conceive you have made a very judicious and eligible choice. A place furnished like Viewfield and possessing such magnificent accommodations is seldom to be met with in Scotland without the appendage of a great territory. The price appears moderate and I imagine you have altogether made a very advantageous purchase. I wish that my Friends had limited their acquisitions of lands for me to an extent similar to that which you have made. No man can afford to buy much land without an extravagant fortune, unless he submits to suffer a diminution of revenue more than he will always find equable. I sincerely hope my dear Grant that your next measure will be to establish a Mistress at Viewfield. I know your sentiments on the subject are judicious and sound."

James replied that his friend's hopes were to be fulfilled.

He brought his parents over from Abernethy to see his estate and to meet his future wife. Parson John was delighted by the prospect of having such a charming daughter-in-law and his wife spread the news amongst the relations.

Aunt Foster in London sent her congratulations and love to the future Mrs JAG. She had always referred to her nephew as "Young JAG" and her brother-in-law as "Uncle JAG". James began to accept that he would be known by this abbreviation within the family, whilst receiving the deferential appellation of James Augustus Grant in public.

James and Elizabeth were married by Parson John at Millbank on 28th April 1813. On the same day Colonel William wrote to his Edinburgh lawyer, Donald Mackintosh, who incidentally was no relation, concerning their marriage settlement –

> *"This will be delivered to you by Mr Grant of Viewfield who you'll see has made choice of my oldest Daughter to pass his days with, in all appearance they will be a happy Couple or I am much deceived -- By reading over this Contract of marriage you'll see he has been most liberal in his Settlements, of which I hope she will retain the most grateful sense while she exists. I am sure I shall. You'll please get the enclosed properly registrated for preservation; the Original has not been keeped as it ought-- Be so Obliging as (to) take care of it till you come North, when I shall rely on the pleasure of seeing you under this roof which at present is rather Confused; tho at all times will be glad to hear of your welfare. Mrs Mackintosh joins me in best wishes to you & believe me with Sincere Regard etc."*

Donald Mackintosh, a bachelor, had a fondness for the Colonel's younger daughter Margaret. Although she addressed him as her dear friend, she did not contemplate marriage to him. Her brother William's wife Jane was having her young sister to stay. William teasingly suggested that the Belles of Nairnshire were eager to throw a Ball for Donald at the earliest opportunity, knowing that he was not altogether comfortable on the dance floor.

Amongst many who sent their congratulations was James's friend and self appointed financial adviser, Charles Forbes. Elizabeth turned out to be a particular favourite of his, much to the advantage of her brother Guyon.

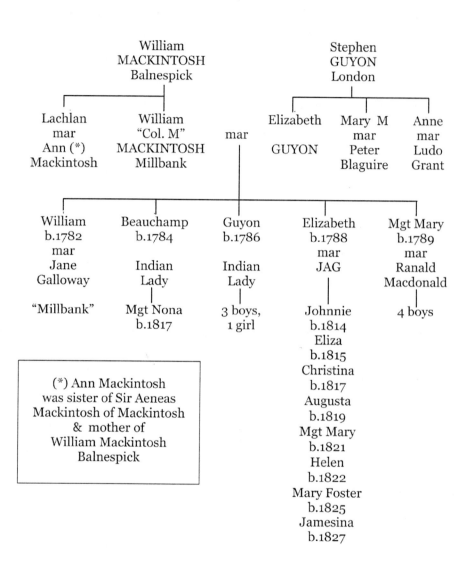

	William MACKINTOSH Balnespick			Stephen GUYON London	

| Lachlan
mar
Ann (*)
Mackintosh | William
"Col. M"
MACKINTOSH
Millbank | mar | Elizabeth

GUYON | Mary M
mar
Peter
Blaguire | Anne
mar
Ludo
Grant |

| William
b.1782
mar
Jane
Galloway

"Millbank" | Beauchamp
b.1784

Indian
Lady

Mgt Nona
b.1817 | Guyon
b.1786

Indian
Lady

3 boys,
1 girl | Elizabeth
b.1788
mar
JAG

Johnnie
b.1814
Eliza
b.1815
Christina
b.1817
Augusta
b.1819
Mgt Mary
b.1821
Helen
b.1822
Mary Foster
b.1825
Jamesina
b.1827 | Mgt Mary
b.1789
mar
Ranald
Macdonald

4 boys |

(*) Ann Mackintosh
was sister of Sir Aeneas
Mackintosh of Mackintosh
& mother of
William Mackintosh
Balnespick

Figure 6 - Mackintosh of Millbank Family Tree

8. The Mackintosh Family

Charles Forbes had for many years looked after the Bombay end of the firm of Forbes & Co. Its head was Charles's uncle, John Forbes, who resided in Fitzroy Square near London's Regent Park, with his office in Devonshire Square. The family originated in Aberdeenshire where they had a property at Ashgrove.

On his way out to India as a seventeen year old, James had carried with him a letter of introduction from Mr Forbes to his nephew, who had taken James under his wing in Bombay before Governor Duncan's arrival a year later. James opened an account with the firm into which his salary was paid. Charles arranged for him to join an underwriting syndicate providing insurance for vessels and their cargoes, which significantly added to his income. As Chief Secretary to the Government, James was later involved in official business with the firm.

The "House" of Forbes & Co, in addition to carrying on trade between India and the UK, acted as bankers for individuals and various organisations including the Government of Bombay. Duncan sought Charles Forbes's advice on a number of trading issues and nominated him as his executor in his will.

The balance in James's account in Bombay had been transferred to his London agents, Porcher & Co via Forbes & Co's London office. Its manager was Mr William Bridgman who kept him informed of developments in the firm. Charles was due to take over from his uncle who was getting on in years with failing eyesight.

Soon after Jonathan Duncan's death, Charles decided to return home. He had issued a circular –

"Am departing for Europe after a long period as senior partner of Forbes & Co. My name and interest will continue in the Firm. Looking forward to the day when my Children may be ranked among members of it. Confident my friend Mr Money will effectively conduct the affairs of the Firm in my place. Trust you will continue your support of the firm."

Walker wrote –

"Your old friend Charles Forbes is reported to have offered £30,000 for the Estate of Ancram not far from this. It is a fine place and altho not intrinsically worth this money will probably sell for more, and more is demanded. You would see by the advertisements in the Papers that Forbes is a candidate to represent Beverly in Parliament. I imagine Thriepland has an intention also of becoming a member and Sir James Mackintosh is said to be canvassing for Nairnshire. If they all succeed we shall have a number of Bombay Senators."

Thriepland had been legal Counsel to the Government and Sir James Mackintosh Chief Judge of the Presidency of Bombay.

It was not long before Charles Forbes made his way northwards to his family home in Aberdeen. He was invited to stay with James and his young wife at Viewfield. He was much taken with Elizabeth and decided to do what he could for her brother Guyon.

Colonel Mackintosh had tried to obtain suitable employment for his sons. William had poor eyesight and could not take up a career in the army. His father spent a lot of money setting him up in firms engaged in cotton spinning, none of which were successful. He was at the present time keeping a low profile from his Glasgow creditors. A commission had been purchased for Beauchamp in the Company's army in Madras. He was a Lieutenant, soon to be promoted Captain. Guyon wished to go to sea. The best the Colonel could do was to get him an appointment as 4th mate of one of the Company's vessels trading with China. He was expected home soon.

Margaret was to stay with an Aunt in Bath and hoped to greet her favourite brother in Bristol on his return. Charles Forbes, after meeting him in London and being impressed with his attitude, thought he could get him useful employment with the firm in Bombay. He paid for his passage out to

India and enlisted his successor Mr Money to help him. There he was to be given a half share in a vessel called "The Mornington" and would set about building up trade between Madras and Padang in Sumatra. Elizabeth must have created quite an impression on Charles Forbes who also was ever ready to help her husband.

Frank Warden who had succeeded James as Chief Secretary also took an interest in Guyon, whom he found to have a refreshing personality. He wrote –

"I had the pleasure of receiving yr letter of 31 Oct last by your Brother-in-law Mr Guyon now Capt McIntosh - he was proceeding to England as an officer of the Caroline I believe, but the Government having determined most opportunely to dispose of the "Mornington" Cruizer a vessel with which you are familiarly acquainted, Forbes & Co purchased her for 80,000Rs and Mr McIntosh has been appointed to her. They have changed her name to the Wellington. I know not how His Excellency the Most Noble the Right Honourable the late Governor General will relish this preference.(The Gov Gen Lord Mornington, later the Marquis of Wellesley, was the elder brother of Arthur Wellesley who had recently become the Duke of Wellington). *Had he been in power in India, he would probably have ordered the whole firm to England for paying so bad a compliment to the Ruler of India and sent Guyon home in chains. Your brother as you may well imagine has been so constantly employed in getting his ship ready that I could not have him at the old House as frequently as I could wish. He will however come again I conclude when I trust that the acquaintance which has*

commenced will ripen into greater intimacy. He has a brother here of the Madras Artillery to whom I have not yet had the pleasure of an introduction".

Mr Bridgman was a ready source of information on the latest coffee house gossip and the goings on in the House of Commons where all were shocked by the assassination of the Prime Minister, Spencer Perceval on the 11th May.

While James had been acquiring Viewfield and courting Elizabeth in 1812, momentous events had been taking place on the continent, which Parson John was eager to relay to his congregation.

Arthur Wellesley, now known as Marquis Wellington, had captured the strategically important fortresses of Cuidad Rodrigo and Badajos inside the Spanish border. The widely separated French armies in Spain, although greatly superior in numbers to the British, could only concentrate against him at the expense of losing control of the provinces from which they depended for their supplies. The siege of Cadiz was raised after three years and Madrid was temporarily liberated. Again Wellington withdrew to positions which suited him and offered battle to the main French army under Marshal Soult, who suffered a humiliating defeat at Salamanca. As the weather deteriorated, both armies subsequently retired to winter quarters.

The French existed in near starvation conditions having denuded, by earlier plunder, most of the surrounding countryside. Napoleon supplied his armies by ruthless confiscation of the produce of those he had conquered. It was to prove a policy which inevitably caused his downfall.

The self-styled Emperor had assembled a huge army for his invasion and subjugation of Russia. It was simply too big to sustain itself by living off the country through which it passed, especially since the Russians adopted a scorched earth policy as they withdrew towards Moscow. As Napoleon prepared for the battle of Borodino which he won at the expense of frightening casualties he learned of Soult's defeat by Wellington at Salamanca. The writing was on the wall. For the most part the Russians followed Wellington's tactics of withdrawing until the French outran their supplies. When they entered Moscow, supposedly in triumph, they found the city deserted. The inhabitants had set fire to everything.

The Russian armies circled round Moscow and obliged the French to begin a disastrous retreat. During the winter of 1812/13 the remnants of Napoleon's once immense army struggled homewards in atrocious conditions.

Before he was assassinated, Perceval had seen no point in openly supporting the Russians as he was in no position to offer them direct support. Despite much opposition he had however been backing Wellington's successful strategy in the Peninsular, which committed a significantly large proportion of Napoleon's armies to the support of his brother Joseph whom he had installed as King of Spain.

Just as the French controlled most of mainland Europe, so Britain, since the battle of Trafalgar in 1805, had controlled the seas. Napoleon decreed that none of his European vassals should trade with Britain and the latter imposed a blockade of their ports. This did not suit the fledgling United States who had been building up trade with the continent. After the British navy intercepted a number of her vessels America lost patience and declared war. As well as resulting in skirmishes on the border with Canada it severely affected trade across the Atlantic. This was partly the cause of William Mackintosh's latest business failure.

William had persuaded his sister Elizabeth to lend him money under a bond. He had been obliged to get his mother to guarantee some of his bills. His father had, on several occasions, drawn on his Forres banker, John Gordon, for cash to pay for some of his son's debts. In his accompanying letters, Gordon referred to the Colonel's health which in the autumn of 1813 was deteriorating.

Elizabeth was concerned and paid regular visits to Millbank, a comfortable ten minute walk. Her visits became less frequent with the approaching birth of their first child.

Their son was born at Viewfield on the 6th June 1814. He was baptised "Sueton John" by the Rev Alexander Grant of Cawdor with whom James had stayed before his marriage. Sueton was a family name of the Grants of Milton and John the name of his grandfather, Parson John. The witnesses were Colonel Mackintosh, Miss Mackintosh (the Colonel's daughter Margaret) and his son William Mackintosh Jnr, all of Millbank.

Parson John had written on the 8 June –

"My dear James
After writing to you yesterday, your daily expected letter & its tidings came here. Glory be to God! for his goodness & may we all be thankful & humble & your wish moderation. I am not going to enlarge. You will readily admit that it would be needless as more is confirmed in our hearts than we can or chose to attempt expressing. We shall expect to have a line or two a little frequently in some few days.

I have acquainted them at Gartinbegg & Tullochgorm & mentioned it to Col Grant as I happened to be writing to him about the fate of poor B's application. This and hearing from poor George & Nelly's coming forward are a collection of providential events at the same time. We send our fond prayers for a continuation of favourable accounts of Mrs Grant's continuing well and free of fever ….."

The baptism had taken place on the 6th July. Less than a fortnight later, on the 18th July 1814, Colonel M died. He had written to Beauchamp informing him of his grandson's birth adding –

"I find myself failing fast--You'll say no wonder if I consider that I am in my Seventy third year of my age and how few lives to this period. "

9. Col M's legacy & abdication of Napoleon

On 19th July William very properly had his father's "repositories" sealed, by William Grant of Seabank, and informed Donald Mackintosh. On 23rd July they were formally opened again to find his will. Having ascertained that his trustees were –

1. Elizabeth, his widow.
2. Sir Aeneas Mackintosh Bart, 23rd Mackintosh of Mackintosh.
3. William Mackintosh of Balnespick, his late brother Lachlan's son.
4. Late David Shirreff, who had married one of Lachlan's daughters.
5. Donald Mackintosh WS Edinburgh, who had drawn up the will.

The repositories were resealed awaiting DM's arrival. On 13th September they were reopened, and Donald spent several days at Millbank sorting the Col's papers, with his widow, William and JAG. Col M's estate basically consisted of –

30,000+ 3% consols value approx	£20,000
Balance with London agents in excess of	£1,673
Balance with his local banker Gordon, Forres	£641
Shares in the Nairn Fishing Company	£100
Insurance policy on the Life of Sir H Mann	£2,500
Crops at Millbank etc	£143

plus interest, less funeral expenses and debts

The heritable property of Millbank automatically went to William.

Mrs Col M was to have 1/3 of his estate in life rent, which was to pass to her children on her death. The other 2/3 was to be divided equally between their 5 children.

There were some small legacies.

It was arranged that William's mother would continue to live at Millbank and pay him the half yearly interest from her 1/3 which Donald Mackintosh was to invest. He took on the office of factor of her trust and set about obtaining probate so that the childrens' portions could be distributed. William was to draw up lists of Creditors and Debtors and to get a valuation of the house furniture and farm stock. He was disappointed that he was not to have a larger share of his father's moveable estate, as his eldest son, but his father had pointed out in his will that he had already been advanced a considerable sum.

James was not involved in the proceedings other than as a representative of his wife, a beneficiary. Affairs dragged on for some years as attempts were made to extract money from the Colonel's London Agents, who had gone into liquidation. The children received an interim payment of £4053 in 1815, and nearly £1,000 more when probate was finally agreed.

Mrs Colonel M died in 1828 but her trust funds were not finally distributed until 1836. Donald Mackintosh's records of all that had happened were to be passed on by his executor to James's wife in 1847. There were many papers giving details of The Colonel's and Mrs Mackintosh's families and their finances which then came to light.

Elizabeth was consoled over the loss of her father, with whom she had been very close, by the daily progress of her new born baby.

Young Johnny's other grandfather, Parson John, had not been slow to broadcast the news of his granchild's birth to the relations in Strathspey and further afield. In addition to congratulations he received more details of the momentous events which had been taking place on the continent which he felt obliged to pass on to his congregation. He had been following the progress of events, in particular concerning Wellington's campaign in Spain since his defeat of Soult at Salamanca.

During 1813 he had cleared nearly the whole of Spain of the French. They only retained an area around Barcelona defended by an army under Marshal Suchet. The Emperor's brother Joseph, whom he had made King of Spain, narrowly evaded capture after overwhelming defeat at the battle of Vitoria, losing all the treasure he and his entourage had accumulated in the previous 5 years. Wellington's army subsequently crossed the frontier bordering the Bay of Biscay and invested the French fortress of Bayonne.

As Napoleon withdrew from his abortive invasion of Russia, Germany and other northern states began to assert their independence from French domination. The Prussians under General Blucher attacked the retreating Emperor who was being hotly pursued by Czar Alexander at the head of a vengeful army. Napoleon had formed an alliance with Austria, cemented by his marriage to crown Princess Marie Louise, after divorcing his wife Josephine. The Austrian Emperor however was persuaded to join the Czar and the King of Prussia in a concerted move to drive the French back across the Rhine.

As the northern allies advanced into France in 1814, Wellington, with his Spanish and Portuguese allies, invaded the south of the country. He drove Marshal Soult eastward, defeating him successively at the battles of Orthez and Toulouse. He had taken special care to see that provisions supplied by the local peasantry were paid for, in stark contrast to the French practice of commandeering the requirements of their army by force without compensation. One of the results of this was the declaration by the people of Bordeaux, the third largest city of France after Paris and Lyon, of their support for the deposed Bourbon royal family and rejection of their forced allegiance to Napoleon. This coincided with the capitulation of Paris to the northern allies. The French senate called for the abdication of their Emperor whom the allies banished to the Island of Elba, off the coast of Italy.

So, after 20 years of war, peace finally reigned in Europe. The three monarchs of Russia, Austria and Prussia were invited to London and entertained lavishly by the Prince Regent.

James later heard from Frank Warden how the news had been received on the 1st August 1814 in Bombay –

"We yesterday received accounts of Bonaparte's having accepted the offer of a pension on condition of his returning to the Island of Elba. I must confess I did not expect this from his proud spirit. I thought he would have fallen on the field of battle, rather than become a pensioner upon the Kingdom he once ruled. Surely he cannot contemplate an opportunity to retrieve his reverses. The world has suffered sufficiently from his inconsiderate & insatiable ambitions and will not be disposed to aid his restoration to power. He must therefore do as other great men are doing, for instance Walker and yourself, rearing cabbages and potatoes in the bosom of retirement. I wish for the sake of example that such a provision had not been made for him. He ought in some degree to have suffered for the ills & the misery which he has entailed upon the world. He ought to have been sent to Corsica and left to his own without means to maintain himself for the remainder of his

life. Colonel Morris, whose character & abhorrence of the Service you must know, thinks that the greatest punishment that could have been inflicted on Bony would have been to send him out a cadet to India".

Warden as well as providing much information about James's former colleagues nearly forgot to mention that –

"We are about erecting a Kirk in Bombay. Should you therefore again cross the ocean you will have no excuse for not attending Divine Service".

Henry Shank also wrote –

"I know not whether I am quite clear whether I may not still hear that you have not entirely relinquished the view of Bombay - from what you express, I still say decidedly that if five years of Council are within your reach I think that you ought to accept most unquestionably - I think you ought even to apply on the score of your long laborious office of Secretary, & I know you would have the support of Mr Grant. I trust Mrs Grant will not be displeased at an old friend in thus offering his advice. You must tell her that we are not very uncivilized Beings here, & positively if you do return, that I look for the pleasure of receiving you under our roof at Belvidere - will you have the goodness to offer our united kindest regards, etc ....."

Whilst James was sure in his own mind that he would prefer to establish himself with his family at Viewfield, he would none the less have liked to have seen more of his many old friends in India.

That he was still highly thought of by the "Direction" was evident from an enquiry he received from William Dalmeida of the Special Committee at East India House on the subject of the improvement of the system of judicial administration established under the Presidency of Bombay.

James submitted his answers to their 13 Questions in a comprehensive reply covering 25 pages. His covering letter read –

"The objects embraced in those queries are of such weighty and serious consideration that I have experienced some embarrassment in stating my answers to them, but I felt I should defeat the purposes of your reference, and disappoint the just expectations to be entertained from my course of service in India, were I to suffer motives of diffidence to suppress the opinions and suggestions which have occurred to me on the very important points to which my attention has been called.

In the want of official records or other useful aids to assist my judgement, some apology will I trust be found for the imperfect state in which my answers are now submitted and, with this explanation, I would request you to do me the favour to bring them to the notice of the Special Committee".

James had, within a few months of his marriage, embarked on his second, much longer, career in Local Government. With a young family and concern for his aged parents, a return to Bombay was not a serious option.

10. Forres Council, Changes, Waterloo

On 22 August 1813 Colonel Francis wrote to James from Cullen House –

> *"My dear Sir*
> *Will you allow me to propose you as one of the Forres Council in place of our friend Tullochgorm who now feels the journey to Forres from Strathspey rather much and has signified to me his wish to resign. With our united best compliments to you and Mrs Grant. Yrs etc."*

Colonel Francis, as procurator for the Earl of Seafield, was patron of the Burgh of Forres, a position which at the time gave him the power to nominate people to the Town Council. Whilst the Baillies or Magistrates needed to be residents of the burgh, the rest of the Council were for the most part landowners in the vicinity. Tullochgorm, who had to travel some 30 miles to attend meetings, was by no means the most distant member. James, living in Nairn, had to travel only ten miles.

It was decided to make him a Burgess of the Burgh. His Ticket, dated 24 September 1813, read -

> *"in favour of James Augustus Grant Esq late Secretary to the Government of Bombay now of Viewfield by unanimous consent of George Grant Esq of Burdyards Provost of the Burgh of Forres, Messrs Alexander Carmichael, Thomas Eddie and Alexander Fraser, Baillies, James Eddie Dean of Guild, William Hayes Treasurer and the members of the Council."*

Inverness, 15 miles on the other side of Nairn from Forres, also decided to issue a Burgess Ticket three weeks later on 15 October 1813 -

"in favour of J.A. Grant of Viewfield Nairnshire in presence of Thomas Gibson Provost of Inverness, Charles Jameson, John Mackenzie, William Chisholm & Farquhar McDonald Bailies, Alexander Mackenzie Dean of Guild & Lewis Grant Treasurer of the Burgh."

News of the arrival of such an eminent person as James in the district had spread far and wide, but he was not made a burgess of his home town of Nairn until four years later.

Alexander Carmichael, the senior Baillie on the Forres Council, had been one of the agents for the sale of Viewfield by Colonel Ludovick Grant in 1807. James was to get to know him well and their families were often in each others company. James's neighbour William Grant was also a member of the Forres Council.

On 21 October 1814, Alex Carmichael wrote –

"Many thanks for your esteemed favour of this date with its inclosure of five Guineas which I shall present to our Trafalgar Club as your subscription. I expected Seabank & you today. I could with difficulty muster up a Majority of Council. You are silent about John. I hope he is getting better. With kindest best

wishes from All to All, I am with much regard my dear sir yours ever truly

A C."

Colonel Francis took a close interest in the affairs of Forres, for which he had recently been Provost. He paid the occasional visit to Viewfield and when Elizabeth received her initial share of her father's estate it was agreed that it be invested by way of a Bond supplied by Lord Seafield. It was common practice to lend money privately to individuals or estates which could provide security and pay interest at a higher rate than the 3% Consols.

Donald Mackintosh invested some of the money of Mrs Colonel M's Trust in this way. Ultimately he laid himself open to criticism for lending trust funds to friends without adequate security, including James's brother-in-law William. The latter was now referred to as Millbank to distinguish him from numerous other William Mackintoshes. He quickly cleared his debts with his share and embarked on some ambitious house-building projects in the vicinity of Nairn.

Beauchamp later wrote to Elizabeth saying that he would have liked to have retired from the Company's service. He was then a Captain but only entitled to a pension of £180pa after 22 years service. He had offered to buy Firhall, but as letters took many months to reach Scotland from his location in central India, the property had been sold by the time his offer arrived. Firhall was situated a mile south of Nairn on the Cawdor road. It had been built out of the proceeds of timber from the fir forests of Rothiemurchus in Strathspey. Beauchamp had passed on Guyons share of his fathers estate to him when he called at Madras in the process of establishing a trading firm plying between that port and Padang on the Island of Sumatra in the Dutch East Indies.

Donald's "friend", Miss Margaret, also of course came into a "fortune" of £4,000. She fell in love with an impoverished Highland farmer called Ranald Macdonald of Gallovie. Governor Mair of Fort George, near Nairn, knew of a number of more eligible bachelors and warned against a liaison with someone of such limited means. He wrote to James –

"My dear Sir
Understanding you have the intention of going some
distance, it is probable we may not have the pleasure
of meeting before we go south. I therefore beg to
express Mrs Mair's & my own best thanks to Mrs
Grant & you for your very friendly attention to our
daughters who were extremely delighted with their
visit to Viewfield. The dear children are in their
estimation such as never had appeared before - God
bless them and may they afford you every possible
enjoyment. They request you will make my
congratulations to Miss Mackintosh, and that every
happiness may attend her expected change in life. I
have not the most distant knowledge of the
gentleman having never before heard of him even by

name but as the match is said to be entirely her own & that it has the perfect concurrence of all her friends I trust she shall be happy for I think her a most amiable young woman and calculated for any man's wife high or low to be perfect. But in all marriage settlements I like the English mode of settling the wife's fortune on herself & to her children. I had a young lady at Aberdeen, the daughter of an Uncle of mine who had some money. Two clergymen thought they had married her well before we came north. The consequence is the mother's money is gone and we have two children of the marriage on our hands without any support. Pardon me my dear Sir for troubling you with this anecdote, as it obtruded on my mind, tho I trust it is in no way connected with the present subject.

Mrs Mair and my daughters desire to unite with me in kind regards & good wishes to Mrs Grant, yourself, Miss Mackintosh & the dear children Yrs etc."

James and Elizabeth had had a second child, Eliza.

The family took great care to prevent Ranald from doing away with Margaret's fortune. Donald Mackintosh drew up a marriage settlement on the lines suggested by Governor Mair by which her money was tied up in trust for her children. She was only able to draw the interest, to support her husband's pressing needs. James along with Millbank and Donald Mackintosh were appointed her trustees.

Charles Forbes was not backward in giving his advice to James on the investment of the balance of his funds which remained after his purchase of Viewfield. It was suggested that India Stock would provide a better return than the 3% Consols (Government consolidated annuities) and would be just as secure. He had given his blessing to the formation of a new firm of Smith, Rickards & Co. Rickards had preceded James as Secretary to the Government of Bombay and wrote –

"Dear Grant.
You will perhaps be surprised to see my name in the accompanying circular, but here I am embarked in a busy scene and with every prospect I am happy to add of profitable as well as pleasant employment. In recollection of our old friendship I send you one of our credentials & shall be happy to render you any service my new occupation may enable me to do in this quarter.

Our friend Bridgman, now is at my elbow, but with being so full of business in consequence of the Cumbria being or thought to be sailing for Bombay, desires me to add with his kind remembrances that he has received your letter of the 29th March & that he will take an early opportunity of answering it with his own pen.
2 George St Mansion House London."

The new firm's credentials dated 14 April 1815 stated –

"We beg leave to acquaint you, that we have established a House of Business in London, which will be conducted under the Firm of SMITH, RICKARDS, and CO, and confined strictly to Agency.

The Members composing this Firm, whose Signatures are annexed, are MR JAMES SMITH, formerly of the House of Forbes, Smith and Co at Bombay; MR ROBERT RICKARDS, late of the Civil Service at the same Presidency; MR WILLIAM BRIDGMAN, of this City; and MR JOHN FORBES MITCHELL, late of the House of Bruce, Fawcett, and Co. at Bombay.

This Establishment having been formed with the concurrence and support of Mr John Forbes, of Fitzroy Square; and of his nephew, Mr Charles Forbes, Head of the House of Forbes and Co at Bombay; we have great pleasure in adding that the latter Gentleman has the option of eventually taking the same place in our Firm.

We beg to assure you of our undivided Attention to such Concerns as may be confided to our Management; and we have the honour to be, Sir your most obedient Servants.

Smith Rickards & Co"

Bridgman wrote to James about the possibility of transferring his account from Porchers –

"My dear Sir
I have already acknowledged the Receipt of your very friendly letters of the 29 March, and 7th Instant and will now endeavour to reply to them.

Nothing appears to me more difficult than to form a prospective opinion of the results of the approaching Contest (Waterloo) with France, though from the manner in which the subject seems to be generally treated, one would think nothing more easy, for it is decided by the coffee House Politicians that the Contest will be severe, but short - and successful. Of its severity, if a Blow is struck in France by the Allies, I have no doubt - but its duration, and ultimate outcome may disappoint many. I am not by any means gloomy in my politics, but I must look at passing Events impartially. I am certainly much flattered by the handsome manner in which you are pleased to mention my literary labours, and can only say, that I will endeavour to deserve the Commendation your partiality has bestowed, and to take care that it awakens a better principle than Vanity.

I accept with thankfulness your congratulations on the Connection I have had the good fortune to form in London under the Commanding Auspices and powerful influence of our good friends in Fitzroy Square. My obligations to the Messrs Forbes are not to be described in a word, to them I owe everything. Were I to relate every instance of disinterested friendship towards me - the benefits derived from the exertion of it - and last, though not least, the benign influence of their avowed countenance and protection, by surrounding me with such friends as Yourself, Messrs Kinloch, Inglis, Wilkinson, Michie Forbes etc etc, I must write a volume rather than a letter. But as it is my Duty, so let it be my strenuous endeavour rather to merit, by my future Actions, the extraordinary kindness of such extraordinary friends, than to invent language to describe that kindness.

93

Accept my dear Sir, my individual thanks for the confidence you are so good as to place in our Establishment, from which you will receive a few lines by this Post. It does not occur to me that the TIME of withdrawing your Concerns from Devonshire Square is very material - the motive I presume is obvious - The friends who influenced you to go there being no longer connected with P & Co, it will not be a matter of surprise that you should follow those friends - and the mode of your communicating your intention with DELICACY, cannot by any one, be better understood than by Yourself. Our terms of doing business will be at least equally advantageous to our Constituents as those of P & Co, and we have determined (which indeed in justice we were bound to do) that such of our friends as may be disposed to transfer their Concerns to our Management, shall not be put to any additional expense for NEW Powers of Attorney, which will of course become necessary for the Receipt of Dividends, Pay etc.

I know not how to answer your question relative to the probable Rise or Fall of the Funds. If the War be long, they must decline, if short, and prosperous, they will most likely rise a good deal at FIRST, say to 66 or 67; but with our heavy debt, and large permanent expense, they cannot I think REMAIN higher than 63 or 65 for many years to come. I bought some India stock to-day at 176. I think you sold at 200.

Your worthy Brother-in-Law Mackintosh is waiting for final orders at Portsmouth. We send them to him this evening, and I hope he will sail tomorrow - his consort, the Caroline has sprung a leak, and will be delayed some days. I assure you I have always derived great pleasure in embracing all opportunities that have been afforded me of being attentive and useful to him.

It would be very gratifying to me to see you in London and to introduce Mrs Grant and Yourself to my Daughter and Son - We shall some day hope to enjoy the pleasure; and in the meantime, though unknown to your Circle, we beg to make the best regards and wishes of our Circle acceptable.

The Messrs Forbes, Smith, Rickards, Forbes Mitchell etc desire to be kindly remembered."

Porcher & Co wrote to James on 7th June 1815 –

"Messrs Smith, Rickards & Co have handed to us your letter of the 29th Ultimo, expressing a wish that we would close your Account Current with us and pay over the Balance to these Gentlemen. In compliance therewith we have now the pleasure to enclose your Account made up with Interest to this day, shewing a Balance in your favour of £1263.13.1 which we have paid to Messrs Smith, Rickards & Co, and we trust will be found correct on examination.

Enclosed we also send you as desired your Certificate from the Bombay Civil Fund, together with the Receipts which there was no occasion to use.

In desiring a transfer of your Concerns to be made to the newly established Firm of Messrs Smith, Rickards & Co it is very satisfying to us to know from you that the management of your Affairs while they have been in our charge has your approbation; and thanking you for the Confidence you have been kind enough to place in us."

Aunt Foster also referred to the coming "contest" in a letter dated 23 Apr 1815 from Ingoldisthorpe Hall in Norfolk –

"My dear Nephew
Ack yr letter with good news of yr son. Yr uncle had a serious scrape, thrown from his horse at Downham near Ely and broke his arm. Foster, Jane (his wife) and I stayed with him at Ely where he was treated by an excellent surgeon before being taken to London for first rate treatment. He mended well but got gout from which he has now recovered. Yr namesake has changed schools and is now at Tunbridge. Mrs Styleman presented the good squire with an heir on the 25th Jan. Had it not been for the frightful reverse on the continent (Napoleon's escape from Elba) he might have begun his long talked of Mansion. Events have damped the spirits of everyone and changed the plans of many. Wish we could have been within reach of Miss Mackintosh(James's S-in-L Margaret). Glad to hear of yr bro's promotion. (George had been appointed Brigade Major at Baroda) *It is slow in India. The two cousins have been fortunate to be made Lieutenants and received kind attention from yr bro. Remember me kindly to Mrs Mackintosh when next you see her* (James's M-in-L)."

Napoleon slipped his minders on Elba at the end of February 1815, landed on the south coast of France and headed for Paris. The leaders of the Allied Powers were attending a congress in Vienna to decide on the distribution of territory in Europe and elsewhere following the restoration of the Bourbons to the throne of France. Napoleon called on the support of his former comrades in arms. As the Bourbons withdrew he took over control of Paris and set out to defeat the allies one by one before they could concentrate their forces against him. His first objective was the Netherlands. Wellington hastily assembled an allied force to the south of Brussels in order to halt the French army while awaiting the help of the Prussian General Blucher.

Rumours abounded of a British defeat but in fact Wellington had withdrawn to a strong defensive position. It was a close run thing until the arrival of Blucher turned the tide and sent the French army into headlong retreat. Napoleon was made prisoner and this time was banished to the British held Island of St Helena in the southern Atlantic, where he could no longer present a threat.

He had been free for 100 days.

James and his friend had spent some time on St Helena on their way home from India five years before. Walker wrote –

> *"The changes that have taken place in Europe have been too rapid almost for reflection and they have been more surprising than all the wonders of a romance. Who could have imagined that Bonaparte would ever have found a residence in St Helena? I hope that there is a sufficient degree of vigour in our political frame that will enable us to pass without*

material injury through all these strange vicissitudes".

As news came in of the Victory at Waterloo on the 18th of June 1815, James's brother-in-law Alexander Grant, his sister Helen's husband, wrote

"What eventful times we live in, and what wonderful changes a day brings about. The present struggle is now likely to be of short duration but it has been a most sanguinary struggle for our poor countrymen".

11. Supporting his Relations

It was generally expected, after Napoleon was forced to abdicate in 1814, and with the ending of war with France and America, that international trade would be revived. The blockade of continental ports which had resulted in war with the United States was no longer necessary. It had severely affected trading with the West Indies. The actions of American privateers had led to the loss of British ships and their cargoes. Alex Grant in common with many other traders in Glasgow was badly affected as his letters to James explained.

In February 1815 he wrote –

"We have been very idle here during winter - little or nothing doing. The return of peace has as yet done us no good but much of the contrary - but were the negotiations at Vienna once finally closed and the limits of the different powers fixed, commercial regulations would follow and the current trade run in the natural way. At present all is in doubt and uncertainty and we must continue so more or less until the arrangements I have mentioned take place. We rejoice to learn Mrs Grant and the young Laird are so well. Our little pair are thriving and your namesake is a most entertaining chattering little fellow. Helen is quite well and unites with me etc.."

By April Alex was in serious trouble –

"My Dear James
... After the favourable account I gave you of my
success in business during the year 1813 - You will
not be prepared to receive from me the painful
communication which I have now to make. During
all last year and this winter the misfortunes in Trade
were numerous beyond precedent. It was not to be
expected I should escape but I had until lately hoped
to have got thro without losing all. When I had got
my engagements reduced to narrow limits, I within
these few days have met with two heavy losses which
paralyse me completely and render the prospect
before me extremely dark.... I dont know what to
do.......My main consideration is the future comfort of
my dear Wife and innocent Babes. It is rumoured
that the factorship of Strathspey may become vacant.
Poor Helen would be agreeable to my taking a
chance at it. I would prefer ease of mind even upon
bread and water to the tormenting anxieties which I
am a prey to. Could you write to Col Francis Grant
on my behalf? Your father could again apply when
my misfortunes can with propriety be made known
to him. Alternatively I might take a farm in
Strathspey. I once turned down an offer but now
think differently. It may be satisfactory for you to
know that the Home we live in is regularly secured to
Helen and her children. I have made my situation
known to no one but yourself".

James would do what he could to help, but his
means were limited. He had already laid out
£10,000 unproductively here and in India.

His assistance would have to be in the form of a loan. How had Alex ended up in his present embarrassed state?

Alex explained that his brokering business at 10/- per cent had contracted with the decline in trade and was not bringing in enough money. He had done some buying and selling on his own account and like most of his fellow merchants in Glasgow had lost money with the general fall in prices. He had also been an underwriter for the past two or three years. The destruction by American privateers had been particularly severe and costly. His brother in Honduras had recently died giving him cause to expect that a debt of £1100 due by him would be repaid from his estate. His executors had been in dispute with others and the decision of the court swallowed everything up. Colonial creditors took precedence and he was left with nothing.

Matters had come to a head with the loss of one of Forbes & Co's vessels en route from the Clyde to Bombay. Another underwriter, taking advantage of a single expression in the insurance policy, had refused to settle the £800 due, leaving Alex to pay the full amount. He would do his best to extricate himself but it was not easy to appear cheerful when his heart was full, but this he was obliged to do for the sake of appearances. His brokerage business had been trifling since the colonies were given up. Trade in this place had halved.

It was agreed that James would become Alex's sole creditor, providing sufficient for him to clear the balance of his remaining debts. James hoped to be repaid in time but would not be an obdurate creditor. The factorships were not a practical possibility so he hoped Alex would come by a suitable alternative.

Alex was much obliged for the handsome and liberal manner in which James had entered into the view of his present situation. His credit was entire and his true situation unknown to the world. Later he was to gain employment from Rothiemurchus, managing the timber which was rafted down the Spey to Garmouth.

James had many requests for help at this time which for the most part involved recommending relations and sons of friends to his former colleagues who were still serving in India. Guyon had created an excellent impression and was welcomed by all his friends there. It was very much an era of patronage.

John Clark, the elder son of Parson John's sister Margaret, was keen to join the army. In 1814 James had tried to promote his career through his friendship with General Nicolls, who had been Commander in Chief of the Presidency's army when James was Chief Secretary of Bombay. He was now retired and living in Lymington, whence he wrote to James –

"I have received your favour of the 16th instant under cover from our friend Mr Charles Forbes, through whom I should have replied, but as there is a recess of Parliament I think it likely he may be Holiday Keeping out of London.

I was not unmindful of your young Friend for I submitted his name to the Commander in Chief as in every way well qualified for a Commission in his Majesty's Service for which I recommended him in the strongest manner and to give it the greater chance I wrote a private letter to Colonel Torrens saying it was a friend of yours that I was applying for and who I very much wished to serve. If my recommendation has the weight I hope and expect, you will see Mr John Clark's name very soon in the Gazette, an Ensign in the 66th Regt. Should that be the case our Depot which had long been stationed at Winchester has within these few days been removed to the Island of Jersey, where he will have to join them. If he does succeed, the letter from the Adj General advising him to join the Regt will probably be sent to me to forward, so that should you see a letter sent to your House from the Adj General's Office, you will know, before you break the seal, we have succeeded".

James received a second letter from Gen Nicolls saying –

"I received the enclosed by this post and forward it without delay. You see it calls for an answer which Mr Clark will address to The Adj General of the

103

Forces, Horse Guards, London, and convey the letter itself to be shewn as directed to the Officer Commanding at Jersey........

Adieu my dear Sir etc

A Nicolls".

Soon after this letter arrived, news came of Napoleon's abdication and banishment to Elba. Recruitment for the army was cut short in anticipation of redundancies in a peacetime army. John Clark had second thoughts and was not sorry to be offered an opportunity of declining his appointment. James had done his best for the young man, of whom he could not bring himself wholeheartedly to approve.

Despite having to cope with his own financial embarrassments, Alex Grant had been trying to help John Clark's younger brother Sweton, who wished to go to sea. In his letter of 28 February 1815 he wrote –

"My dear James
The ladies [their wives] *have exchanged all the news. Note the Clarks are allowing their son Sweton Clark to pursue a career of his choice* [to go to sea]. *I will do what I can but there are no ships available at present. It is a pity the Clarks did not come to this decision three months ago. It will be May before there is likely to be a ship with such a Captain as I could wish. Almost all our regular trading West Indiaman are at present out upon their Voyages. A small fleet came home last month and there is another small one just now waiting a wind outward. McGeorge with*

whom I should much like to place him does not go out again this year. The Diana has been sold, and another Ship bt in London to replace her, which McGeorge was offered to command but he remains at home for a Voyage, to go thro a course of treatment for a bad scurvy which he got two years ago out of a Prize he took, and which he has never been able to get rid of. The next fleet will not be home before the end of April and may again sail sometime in May. Likely however by that time they will sail single ships. I shall by that time have sufficient opportunity of placing him in a situation to my mind. In the meantime, if the Schoolmaster at Nairn has any knowledge of Navigation, would it not be proper that he employs that short interval to get some smattering of that Science and indeed Geography would be also of considerable service. After he goes to sea he will have very little opportunity of improving himself.... Much preparation will not be necessary. A few sailors clothes and shirts which can be got ready here or at Greenock. Anything expensive or fine would be thrown away while at sea".

In June he wrote –

"My dear James
Still trying to accommodate Sweton Clark... The packet which arrived two days ago brings accounts that the News had reached the Islands of the probability of a War with France [following Napoleon's escape from Elba] and that in consequence the Admiral on the Station had ordered that no vessel should sail without convoy. A convoy was expected to sail about the 20th May which may be looked for by the middle of next month. I continue to look out for a suitable ship (I mean Captain) for

poor Sweton Clark. I have several in view in the next convoy. The ships outward cannot be expected to sail before the first or second week in August".

On the 23rd August 1815 Alex wrote –

"My dear James
I have engaged Sweton Clark for the Ship Westmoreland - Captain Hamlin - a regular trader to Demeraray from this port, and the property of Messrs Campbell, Hamilton & Co. They have fixed the period of her departure earlier than I expected say 5th prox, so there is no time to be lost in despatching him on receipt of this, so as he may be here on or before that date. His sea clothes and other articles for the voyage he will get best here, so that no delay needs take place in the way of outfit. The terms are - to be indented for three years during which period he will be allowed from £24 to £25 in all, by way of supplying him with clothes. This period of apprenticeship is required by law to give protection against impress, and no young man is considered a seaman until he has served so long. At the ending of his apprenticeship he should be qualified for the situation of second mate & this, if he is deserving, which I have no doubt he will, I trust we shall have no difficulty in obtaining for him in the Employ he has commenced.

As William Mackintosh mentioned before he left this, that you had some intention of setting out for Abernethy on the 24th, I have also thought it proper to address a few lines for you there, that no time may be lost. Should he not be here by the 5th, there is another ship, the Unicorn, belonging to the same House sails for Jamaica on the 10th, but the former I would prefer. He will of course come by the Inverness coach to Perth, and immediately upon his arrival at Perth he will find a coach ready to start for Glasgow which he should be directed to enquire for the moment he alights. If the weather is fine, he will be as well and cheaper outside, as none of these coaches travel at night. When he comes here let him come direct to this House, No 15 Gordon Street. Helen and our little ones are in their ordinary. She unites with me in kindest regards to you and Mrs Grant and little Johnny etc".

On the 6th October Alexander Grant wrote –

"My dear James.
Being uninformed as to the particular time you proposed leaving Strathspey, and there being nothing pressing that required me writing to you, I have delayed until I could calculate upon your being at home, informing you of my proceedings with regard to Sweton Clark. No doubt he himself would have written previous to his sailing which was delayed for some days by some disturbance among the Seamen of the Port, about rate of Wages - When he arrived here he had £30 in money remaining, and I have contrived to fit him out with Sea Clothes and Sea Bedding, sufficiently complete so as to leave £20 remaining, this with the £25 of wages which he is to receive, £6 first year, £8 the second and £11 the third, puts £45 at his disposal to keep himself in Clothes for the period of his apprenticeship, which will be amply sufficient. I am much pleased with Captain Hamlin, and I have requested him to do every thing for the young man that he can with propriety do without giving umbrage to others. There are two decent young men apprentices in the Ship, one a clergyman's son. The owners have also made a similar request to Captain Hamlin which I doubt not

107

will have its due weight. Everything further rests with himself and he appears to me to have good dispositions, and a determination to persevere with what he has embarked in. The Westmoreland calls at Madeira for wine, and it's probable he may write from thence for the satisfaction of his family.

Helen and the children are in their ordinary. We hope Mrs Grant has not been the worse of travelling from Abernethy. We shall look anxiously for good accounts of her from time to time. Helen will write her sister by Mr & Mrs Mackintosh, now proprietors of the Grove and to be your neighbours".

Not long after returning from visiting Abernethy, James and Elizabeth announced the birth of their second child, Eliza, at Viewfield on the 8th of November 1815. The witnesses at her baptism on the 5th of December were her grandmother Mrs Colonel Mackintosh, her great aunt Miss Mary Grant, William Millbank and his wife Jane, and a Major King.

One of the first persons to be told the good news was James's Aunt "Foster". Her husband , Uncle George Grant, was now retired, after a lenghthy career at the Headquarters of the Honourable East India Company. A painting of their recently renovated building is shown opposite.

1815 had been an eventful year.

Figure 7 - HQ of the HEIC Leadenhall Street

12. Post-war Paris & Prince Leopold

As the Bourbon Monarchy became re-established in France wealthier inhabitants of England took to holidaying there, including the family of James's Uncle George Grant and Aunt Foster. The latter wrote to him from Paris on the 4th of January 1818

"My dear Augustus
It is useless to say how many times I have determined to thank you for your last kind letter, the date of which, and the so friendly wishes expressed in it to hear from me occasionally, greatly, severely, reproach me on re-perusing it this Morning; however if any amends can be made, I am determined it shall be the first letter I write this Year. Should I not receive a speedy reply and such a one as will bring good accounts of you all, I shall have difficulty in forgiving myself for such continued procrastination. Many events may have occurred in the North since you wrote, but still as you had a direction to me here I think you would have sent a letter if there had been anything particularly interesting.

I could scarcely have believed it possible that you should not have heard of our having left England till I received your letter. Your Uncle feels the comfort of having his family about him and never was in better health. Indeed when we consider how many we are, we have great reason to be thankful. Except dear Susan we are all well but she has had frequent returns of the nervous complaints I mentioned to you during the year and the last three weeks has had a more severe attack than any except the first, but is now thank God recovering.

Mrs Foster added another Boy to her group the 18th July who his mother's Aunt desires might be called Nathaniel Watts. He is the stoutest of all her children and she had a better time and more speedy recovery than on any former confinement. Mrs Foster lost her Uncle in the Spring very suddenly; and about three months ago her father had a paralytic stroke, from which I fear he is but imperfectly recovered; though he has been able to write to her, he has not yet found himself able to go out even in a carriage. These are comparatively young people to our relatives in the North, but their constitutions are not as strong to struggle with complaints to which poor human nature is liable.

I was much grieved to hear that your sister & her children were returned to your Father's. Business seems again to have revived, and I would fain hope her Husband will again be able to follow his business which was at one time very flourishing. Your father is a wonderful man of his years. Mrs Forbes has been so many years an invalid that it would appear her constitution and mind are resigned to it. We were glad to hear the Major's wife was better for her journey South, & wish it had taken place before we left England, that I might have had a chance of seeing her. The Autumn of 1817 was so mild I hope your Aunt Bellintomb has escaped the rheumatism this winter. I hope Mrs G Forbes was better for spending the Winter at Aberdeen. Those repeated attacks of her fever complaint must weaken her very much.

Your brother George seems to have the family complaint in his fingers. He scarcely ever writes. It must greatly add to the comfort of Mrs Col McIntosh to have her daughter settled happily so near her. You had I hope an abundant harvest in the North. Last *season nothing could be finer than the crops of corn here.*

You will perhaps be surprised to find that we are still in this city. The fact was we remained in it owing to the illness of poor dear Augusta till we began to think we should all like it better than going farther south, and after making many inquiries in provincial towns, there appeared some objection to each. We then set about in earnest looking for a House here and were so fortunate to meet with one at the extremity of the City next Mont Martre with a garden which was not too large to have wholely to ourselves, which, by taking for the term my own house is let for, we have on very moderate terms. We entered it on the 1st July and found the garden into which the drawing room opens most agreeable during the warm weather. Mrs Foster was in it at the end of a fortnight when she lay in. I hope your good lady had as good a time and the little stranger is thriving.

The Public Credit in this Country appears every day to gain ground, and their present King is warmly attached to our Island, and lived in it long enough to admire and now endeavour to establish some of its laws in his own Kingdom, which in time he will perhaps be able to accomplish; they have tried hard to establish the liberty of the press but that must be a work of time. The Funds give great interest and many of the Emigrants who have till lately left their money in our hands are now recalling it and placing it in their own. I greatly admire the police here, which certainly keep the lower orders of people in much better order than with us. You scarcely ever see a person in the streets in a state of intoxication. If they are, they are immediately taken to the Guard House till in a state to appear with decency. By this means there never are any rows in the streets and at night after 10 o'clock you scarcely see a common person out.

Your namesake is now six feet high & the Medical Men here tell him he will grow three inches more - which I regret as I think six feet quite high enough. We all write in kindest regards collectively and individually to you and all our connections in the North and I remain your most affectionate Aunt ..."

She adds –

"What a grievous loss has our country sustained in the poor Princess Charlotte and her Babe.

When you answer this, direct for me under la Rochefoucault Chaussee D'Antin Paris No 18, and inclose it in a cover to 'JP Grant MP, Sergeants Inn Fleet Street London'. All our letters come from thence and we get them in the Ambassador's bag. This is entre nous. Ours go in the same way to London so you have only the postage from London to pay".

Alex Grant eventually closed down his business in Glasgow and brought his wife Helen and the children to stay at the Manse of Abernethy while he sought employment locally. Many years before, he had made the acquaintance at dances of the lady who was now married to the Laird of Rothiemurchus. Her husband was pleased to offer him the position of Woods Manager with special responsibility for disposing of the rafts of timber which were floated down the Spey to Garmouth, where the river entered the Moray Firth. Alex revived the old custom whereby the Lairds wife was paid a small sum for each raft that reached its destination.

The house in Glasgow, which was in Helen's name, was let and the family found a house to rent in Garmouth.

The Mrs Forbes referred to by Aunt Foster was Uncle George's widowed sister who stayed with her son Major Forbes at Inverernan in Strathdon. Aunt Ballintomb was actually a first cousin of Parson John's. She and James's mother were close friends and the children adopted her as their aunt. The farm of Ballintomb lay on the banks of the Spey opposite Abernethy, below its confluence with the River Dulnain.

James always enjoyed getting letters from his Aunt Foster who for once called him Augustus instead of the usual JAG. She was well in with the Ambassador and characteristically made use of the diplomatic bag. She had commented on the fate of Princess Charlotte and her babe.

When the Monarchs of Russia, Austria and Prussia were invited to London by the Prince Regent to celebrate the first overthrow of Napoleon a young officer in the Prussian entourage, Prince Leopold of Saxe Coburg had paid court to the Prince Regent's daughter and heir, Princess Charlotte, and proposed to her. His offer was rejected because it was intended that she should marry "Slender Billy", the Prince of Orange who was on Wellington's staff. He was to become King of the Netherlands. Charlotte took a dislike to him and the prospect of spending her days in Holland. The dislike was mutual and their engagement was finally terminated the following year. Prince Leopold was encouraged to return to London where he married his Princess. They were very popular and there was widespread grief when she died in childbirth. Her baby did not survive, and the Prince Regent was left with no heir.

In 1830 when France sought to annex the Belgian Provinces which demanded independence from Holland, they were created a separate Kingdom and Prince Leopold was set on its throne. His nephew Prince Albert was to marry Queen Victoria.

In 1819 Prince Leopold carried out a goodwill tour of the North of Scotland and received the Freedom of Forres at the hands of the Provost, who gave his Aunt Foster a first hand account of the proceedings and enclosed an extract from the Forres Gazette describing the event.

PRINCE LEOPOLD'S RECEPTION AT FORRES AND PRESENTATION TO HIS ROYAL HIGHNESS OF THE FREEDOM OF THE BURGH 2D SEPT 1819.

On Thursday the 2d of September 1819 Prince Leopold accompanied by the Marquis of Huntly and the gentlemen of his Royal Highness's suite, visited Forres en route for Grant Lodge and Gordon Castle. On the approach of the Illustrious Stranger a Royal Salute was fired from Trafalgar Tower, while the cheers and acclamations of a large concourse of Spectators testified the interest excited by the Prince's presence. His Royal Highness arrived at Macleans Hotel a little after 1 o'clock and was received at the door by the Provost, Magistrates and Town Council; the Clergy of the Presbytery of Forres, and a numerous Assemblage of Gentlemen. Refreshments suited to the occasion had been provided, and were served up. During his stay His Royal Highness was presented by the Provost J.A.Grant of Viewfield with the Freedom of the Town, which he accepted very graciously. About 2 o'clock the Royal Visitor departed amid renewed cheers from the crowd surrounding the Hotel - all anxious to manifest their attachment to a Prince so justly endeared to the whole British Nation.

At the Levee held during the Princes' stay - the Provost observed to the company assembled, that, impressed with a due sense of the honor conferred upon the Burgh by the presence of so illustrious a Stranger - he would beg to propose his Royal Highness' health in a bumper. The King and other appropriate Toasts followed, after which Mr Grant as Provost addressed the Prince as follows:

"In the name of the local authorities, I have the honor of presenting to your Royal Highness the Freedom of the Town of Forres, which I humbly hope your Royal Highness will be graciously pleased to accept as the only token of Respect and attachment which it is in their power to bestow; nor can they ever fail to appreciate the virtues which adorn your Royal Highness' character, or cease to bear in remembrance the distinction conferred upon this ancient Burgh by the presence of so illustrious a Stranger."

His Royal Highness in reply expressed the great satisfaction with which he received so gratifying a compliment from the Authorities of the Burgh, and begged the Provost to convey as he was pleased to say "in better language than he could use" his warmest acknowledgements to the Town Council. He also testified his pleasure at the distinguished reception he had experienced from all classes.

James had been elected Provost of Forres for a three year term on the recommendation of Col Francis and was to hold that office for two more terms at intervals in the future.

Prince Leopold had also passed through the neighbouring town of Nairn on his journey from Inverness to Elgin. The Pole Road linking the High Street to the Inverness Turnpike was subsequently renamed "Leopold Street". In addition to serving on the Forres Council James was also a member of the Nairn Burgh Council. He was given a Burgess Ticket in 1817 in favour of James Augustus Grant of Viewfield with the unanimous consent of the

Provost, Bailies, Dean of Guild, Treasurer and Town Council of Nairn.

James was an accomplished speaker and adept at composing loyal addresses on behalf of both Burghs as occasion demanded. Although the business of the Council was parochial compared with that with which he had been involved as Government Secretary, he enjoyed carrying out his duties. He gained the reputation for diplomatically getting things, that were necessary, done. He was appointed a JP for Nairn and as a former Judge administered local justice in a firm but understanding way.

Aunt Foster had referred to the lower orders and common persons, naturally considering her family, if not of the aristocracy, certainly of the upper or ruling class. The class divide was a fact of life, but James believed as did his father that all men were equal in the sight of God. You should make full use of any talents with which you were blessed and if this placed you in a position of influence then you had a duty to dispense your power to the common good. In his father's parish there were many desperately poor "objects" for whom weekly collections for the poor fund were made.

James was President of the Nairn Poor Fund Committee which in June 1817 received a contribution of £35 from the Nairnshire Meeting in

London. The Secretary/Treasurer of the Meeting was Isaac Ketchen who wrote –

"Gentlemen
I am directed by the Committee of the Nairnshire Meeting to authorise you, or your Treasurer in your behalf, to draw on me at par for the sum of £35 (thirty five pounds), the amount of sundry subscriptions by the Members of the Nairnshire Meeting and their friends - to aid the laudable purposes you have planned for the relief of the most distressed and deserving poor in your town & neighbourhood - and which plans have been executed during the severity of bad winter, with such good effect to the relief and comfort of many destitute families.

The Committee would have offered this small assistance at an earlier period, did they not consider that it would prove more acceptable when your fund may be supposed nearly exhausted, and at this period, when necessaries of life are usually more scarce & dear than at any other season.

The Committee fully sympathise in your generous & disinterested offices, and have only to regret that from particular circumstances they are not enabled by a larger remittance to shew more decidedly their sincere good will.
I have the honor etc."

James, in the name of the Committee for the Relief of the Poor, sent the Committee's cordial thanks for such judiciously timed benevolence and added that Captain Rose, the Treasurer of the poors' fund, would shortly draw upon Isaac Ketchen at par to the order of Robert Falconer for the amount referred to.

The following paragraph appeared in the Inverness Journal –

"We learn, with great satisfaction, that the members of the Nairnshire Meeting in London have, by a late communication from their Secretary and Treasurer, placed at the disposal of the Committee for the Relief of the poor in Nairn, the sum of £35; an aid regarded as at once so bountiful and seasonable, and so much in unison with former manifestations of liberality, as to entitle the humane Donors to the grateful acknowledgement of the Community."

13. Casting his vote in London

One of the "Nairnites" in London who contributed was William Storm. His father, William senior, after carrying on a successful business in the city, had retired with his wife to his roots in the Fishertown of Nairn. His two sons John and William had succeeded him and undertaken a number of commissions for Colonel and Mrs Mackintosh, with whose children they had grown up. John used regularly to visited Mrs Colonel M's sister Mrs Peter Blaguire in Hampstead. Soon after James returned from India, John went out to Bengal and started a successful business in Calcutta.

William remained in the City and was involved in transferring the Colonel's investments to his widow's trust and to his children.

He was keen to follow his brother to India and sought James's help in obtaining Free Merchants Indentures. These would enable him to trade on his own account independently of the East India Company.

Alexander Walker still compared notes about their young families. He congratulated James on the birth on 8th June 1817 of his second daughter, Christina. He also wrote –

"You would see that John Morris has at last got into the Direction. He is an extraordinary example of the power of perseverance; for it is that only that has brought him in, contrary to the conviction of his unfitness by those who have given him their vote".

John Morris had signed, as Chief Secretary, the letter appointing James to be Private Secretary to Governor Duncan twenty years ago. He decided to write to him on behalf of William Storm. Morris regretted that he was unable to help.

Charles Forbes, now Sir Charles Bart, offered James his advice –

"Whilst you are well known and have influence in the Highlands it counts for little in London. Although you have I hope some sincere and disinterested friends who would cheerfully go to NAIRN to do you an act of kindness, yet their number must be few and in the course of nature they will soon be fewer. Be assured Grant that you must shew yourself a little in this selfish world if you would not be altogether forgotten and overlooked. You must also have something to give to others in exchange for what you may ask, and this you will find in your late application to John Morris, who is, I suspect like most others, once they have got into the Direction; but if he finds you can come up six hundred miles to vote for or against him as the case may be, he will be more receptive to your requests. The greater the inconvenience and sacrifice, the greater the favor conferred....".

James kept his friend's advice in mind. As a shareholder of "Indian Stock" he was entitled to vote in elections for Directors.

There were no proxy votes. They had to be cast in person. Towards the end of the year he was approached by his friend David Inglis, who was a member of Charles Forbes's firm in Bombay when James first arrived in India.

David had recently taken over from Rickards in the firm of Smith, Rickards & Co which was now called Smith Inglis & Co.

He sent James a prospectus from Leamington, setting out the claims of William Money for election to the Direction of the East India Company. Money had taken over as senior partner in Forbes & Co, Bombay when Charles Forbes returned home. He had been instrumental in providing Guyon with his vessel the "Mornington" or "Wellington" as it was now named, and since the start of James's career had shown him much kindness. Whilst taking the waters at Leaminton Spa Charles Forbes and David Inglis were coordinating Money's campaign and canvassing on his behalf. (Sir Charles told James that Mrs Inglis had just brought her husband their seventh child, a boy).

On the 16th of December Money himself wrote to James from the City of London Tavern −

"My dear Sir
A vote or two may decide whether or not I will be
elected as a Director of the East India Company. I wd
appreciate your coming to vote for me".

He enclosed a letter from Sir Charles which read –

"My dear Grant
If I could bring myself to propose to you to come up
and vote for our friend Money at the India House on
the 30th instant I would say that you could not do
anything more acceptable to very many of our
mutual friends. I shall only add that the Contest is
severe beyond example and may be decided by a
single vote. Money is however the favorite and I
should like to see you on the winning side. Mitchell
and my sister are in London. Many of your friends
are hoping to see you, amongst others John Smith
was just now anxiously expressing himself so. With
kind regards to Mrs Grant and best wishes to the
Bairns etc."

James replied –

"My dear Forbes
I received yesterday your letter of the 16th and I
hasten to assure you that God willing I shall be at the
India House on the 30th. I could not endure the
reflection that I had failed to manifest a due interest
in so good a cause. On a similar occasion two years
ago I mentioned to you that there was no man in
whose behalf I should feel more disposed to
undertake the long journey than the respected friend
who has now solicited my vote. Thank him and Inglis
for their letters and say to them that I shall set out by

the Mail this evening. With every good wish etc."

On the 29th December Charles Forbes wrote from Fitzroy Square to James at Miller's Hotel in Jermyn Street –

"My dear Grant
I am most happy to learn your safe arrival. I did not receive your note till late last night or I should have called upon you. I hope however to have that pleasure about eleven this morning, and our mutual friend Mitchell will probably accompany me.

Your favor of the 22nd reached me yesterday morning and afforded us all great pleasure. It is like yourself. I read it to my worthy Uncle and then gave it to him to take to the Committee, being myself poorly, with a severe cold and not able to go to the City early. You have, I am aware, made a great sacrifice of feeling and comfort upon this occasion, but the obligation is the greater upon Money and his friends and we are all most thankful to you, particularly when we contrast your experience with that of some friends who grumble at coming a hundred miles for the like purpose. I have every confidence that you will have the gratification of supporting the successful cause - but the contest is severe. I offer two to one however on the result 100 to 50 that Money comes in - not yet taken.

Sir Robert Barclay arrived from Banff the day before yesterday, Capt Brown formerly of the Duncan from Edinburgh, Crow is coming from Wales and Iveson and Fearnley-Smith expected today. Good night or rather good morning my dear Grant etc."

With such support Money was elected but by the narrowest of margins, and later sent his thanks to James –

"My dear Sir
I much regretted that the state in which I was at the time of my election and for a week afterwards, while confined in Town, did not admit of my seeking you to express more forcibly than I did at the fleeting opportunity once afforded me, the deep sense I entertained of your very great kindness in coming so far, at such a season and at the sacrifice of your personal convenience and domestic comfort, to give me your support at a Crisis so important to my interests. Believe me my dear Sir I shall ever retain a most pleasing and grateful recollection of this strong instance of your friendship, and it adds much to my gratification to think that while you moved from such a distance to help me, you were powerfully induced to do so by your regard for the wishes of our mutual and excellent friends Forbes and Inglis.

After such a journey it will be a source of satisfaction to you to believe that the known intentions of our warm Indian friends operated most seasonably as an example to others and the happy consequence was that, to the force supplied by the distant votes with their hearty zeal I owed my election.

My health is still in a feeble state, but by rest and quiet and country air I am gradually recovering my strength. Mrs M unites with me in the tender of our best respects to Mrs Grant to whom we are much obliged for sparing you and I am etc".

James enjoyed meeting many old friends and in particular William Bridgman with whom he had so often corresponded but never met. He took the trouble to forward as speedily as possible letters to and from James to Beauchamp, Guyon and his brother George (whom Aunt Foster accused of having the family complaint in his fingers).

Elizabeth was very pleased to welcome him home after a fortnight's absence. Their fourth child Augusta was born on the 14th of October 1819.

The following year James's support of his friend bore fruit. He asked William Money if he could help William Storm. He replied from Bath –

"My dear Sir
I must beg you to excuse me for this late acknowledgement of your letter which I had the pleasure of receiving when in a journey in Herefordshire. Expecting at that time to be soon in London I delayed writing till I could ascertain if it would be in my power to comply with your wishes. A troublesome illness with which Mrs Money was afflicted detained me longer than expected, but when I came to London I expected that I should see Mr Storm at the India House next week, however, when I go there I will write and request him to come to me, and I shall be very happy if in my power to obtain the object he wishes. It will always afford me pleasure to forward any purpose in which you take an interest. Yrs etc".

After an interview with William Storm, William Money made the appropriate enquiries and found that he could arrange matters to his satisfaction. He did not have time to advise James immediately but later wrote to him from East India House –

"My dear Sir
I have rested on Mr Storm's acquainting you that I have succeeded in procuring for him Free Merchant's Indentures and therefore being pressed by occupation at the time I delayed writing to inform you. I can truly say as on this and as on every future occasion I shall take pleasure in executing any wish of yours. I am etc".

On the 2nd January 1821 William Storm wrote to James from Hythe –

"My dear Sir
I know not how to express my thanks sufficiently for your kindness nor how I can repay the obligation you have conferred upon me.

Your letter to Mr Money has obtained me Free Merchants Indentures and I am much indebted to him for the handsome manner in which he gave it to me.

Various circumstances had contributed to prevent me from calling upon Mr Money as you requested but he had not forgotten your application and on his coming to town he desired to see me. In about three weeks afterwards he put into my hands the usual documents and when I have named my ship they will be completed.

This act of kindness I shall never forget and trust I may have it in my power to evince my sense of gratitude more effectively than in words.

I have not yet fixed the period of my departure but it is more than likely, if I meet with a ship which I like, sailing the latter end of this or beginning of next month, that I shall then proceed to Bengal. I need hardly say that if I can be of any use to you it will afford me pleasure.

I came down here to spend my Christmas with some friends but return to town in about a week.

I beg my kindest regards to Mrs Grant and wishing you all many merry Christmases and happy new years, I am My Dear Sir, Yours very sincerely

Willm Storm".

Over the years James was to have frequent dealings with William and his brother John. He kept an eye on their parents and helped out their aunts. John corresponded regularly with Beauchamp and Guyon. He occasionally met the latter when his ship called at Calcutta.

In July 1822 John Storm wrote from that city –

"My dear Sir
I beg you will kindly overlook my not having long since addressed you and attribute my silence to any other cause than want of gratitude. Allow me now to offer my sincere thanks for the unmerited favor you so readily conferred on my Brother, and the condescending attention you are pleased to pay to

my poor old parents. My Brother certainly had not interest to have procured the Company's permission to come here through any other channel, and I assure you the favor has not been bestowed on one who is not fully sensible of it.

On his arrival here there was nothing in immediate prospect for him and being desirous of seeing the Eastern Islands he was induced to proceed with a small adventure in that direction and to learn. It is expected to turn out well, for with the latter country there has been very little communication for several years past. He sailed from here in February last. I have heard of his being well on the 19th April at Tringanos where he had touched in the way up the Gulph. He would reach his Post in all that month; Would remain there probably during May and June, and it would take him all July to get back to Singapore or Batavia against the Monsoon. I expect to hear of him from either of these places in the first week of September. There are many circumstances to make me very anxious for his arrival back.

As to my poor parents. I hope you will bear with the little occasional trouble they may give. I am sure they will be as little troublesome as possible - and in all probability it will be of short duration.

Although a stranger personally, allow me to subscribe myself Yrs very sincerely

John Storm."

14. Appointed DL for Nairnshire

When it became known that James was prepared to cast his vote even though he lived 600 miles away, he was much in demand at election time. Tiring of making polite excuses when solicited for his support, he decided the sensible solution was to sell his shares in the Company thereby giving up his right to vote. He did not anticipate that any more of his special friends would aspire to become a Director. By the time Henry Shank returned home some time later and unexpectedly put himself up for election, he had sold his shares and regrettably could not vote for him, which he would otherwise have been only too willing to do.

He did not enjoy applying to his friends for patronage unless they made it clear that it would be a pleasure to help him. In that case he would put himself out for a deserving person who otherwise had little chance of advancement or relief. It was much easier just to supply introductions to former colleagues who were still in India. The process presented an opportunity or excuse to exchange news with them.

His chief correspondents were Henry Shank and Francis Warden in Bombay. Dr Milne also wrote from Baroda with news of his brother George, in August 1819.

"My most worthy and excellent Friend.

Had I been constituted a Planet which you know possesses a diurnal rotary motion, I could not have had more urgent demands made on my powers & facility of changing place than has been made on me since the end of the year 1815, when I broke ground at Poonah for Surat, thence in 6 months for Baroda - thence in a few months for Jerode - thence for Palampoor to hunt Bheils - thence again to Baroda - thence into Malwa & Mewar - thence back again to Baroda - thence to Poonah - thence into Cutch - thence again to Baroda, where I trust I will be permitted to continue to revolve for some time without being obliged to change my orbit. This change of sphere you well know is not favourable to industry & particularly to that species of it, letter writing, because constant change of place brings a degree of unsteadiness & a restless feel with it, not calculated to promote a fixed attention to any object which correspondence with distant Friends requires. But I now take up my pen in reply to your much esteemed & kind letter of the 16th Dec 1817, with great delight.

I have repeatedly, in imagination, transported myself into your society where I hope you will have the Man before many years. I have traversed, both in the East & in the West the various scenes which have passed under our review, from the Bussora Wall to the Assembly Room at Peterhead, where our sojourn was interrupted by the sudden indisposition of my Poor old Father. We have since taken opposite tracks, I from necessity, you from possessing the means of having a choice, & as that choice has contributed so essentially to your happiness, it will be an object of lively interest to me to have the pleasure of visiting that scene, & to witnessing the interesting young

132

shoots which now surround & adorn the parental trunk.

Although in a revolving state during the last campaign, I did not resemble the rolling stone - On my return from the Field I found I had collected a considerable portion of moss, & the Government was pleased to make a very handsome addition to it. I am therefore on the high road to obtaining a comfortable independence which only aims at enabling me to keep my head & feet dry in your wet & chilling climate.

You are now surrounded with an interesting Family, & happy in the enjoyment of that retirement, which is the aim & object of us all, & to which your merits so signally entitle you: and which your kind & amiable disposition is so well calculated to promote & sweeten.

But alas! The numbers of my grey hairs begin to rise up in judgement against me. My limbs which were formerly agile, & my spirit alive to every object of amusement, now, move not, nor thrill not, as in days that have been; & time has strangely depicted his advances in a countenace, which once bore the stamp of youth & of animation.

My residence here is the next door to your Brother. I made him acquainted with your anxious wish of hearing from him at times. He has not been in very good health for some months, & he is not very obedient to the recommendation which has been repeatedly urged, of taking a trip to the sea coast, which he absolutely requires. He has been so long stationary, that a change will be of the greatest service to him. The late arrangements at Baroda have made his situation very handsome. He is now Assistant Quarter Master General to that Force.

You have no doubt perused with great interest the detailed accounts of the late operations of our armies in the East, which have now completely overturned the Mahratta Power, & destroyed their host of plunderers & the Pindarees. The fidelity & bravery of the Bombay Troops have been in several instances signally displayed in the late contest, particularly at Poonah & at Korygaum.

You must have heard of the appointment of Mr Elphinstone to be our Governor on the departure of Sir Evan. Expectation runs high, but I fear he will not be able to maintain himself on the eminence on which the public have already placed him. The disappointment to Sir John Malcolm must have been very great, & some think that Sir John would have been the more desirable Man of the two. Under either of them however, Bombay will no doubt benefit.

You will remember a proposition I formerly laid before you on my return from the Gulph of Persia in 1804, of occupying the Island of Baharain. That measure is now determined on & a Force, consisting of 5,000 Men is ordered to be in readiness to proceed thither after the monsoon, for the avowed purpose of destroying the Jawassimie Pirates, but two Corps are to be left there to prevent their future deprivations, & the Imam of Muscat has agreed to subsidize them.

The Turks have made themselves masters of the Centre of the Desert, so that a very desirable track is now opened of carrying on an easy & direct intercourse with Egypt & Syria; & this extension of the power of the Turks will under our guidance, give a degree of stability to their Empire, & enable them the better to resist the advances of Russia in Asia.

I now want our Government to establish themselves in Abyssinia in order that we on our part have a check on the power of the Turks; for although it is not probable that they will ever cordially join with Russia against us, or have the means singly of disturbing us, Russia may have it in her power to employ compulsion, & we ought to be prepared to check them by entering Egypt & conquering Syria.

I must now conclude by repeating my warmest & best wishes for your health & happiness, & that your amiable partner & Family may continue an honor to your many virtues, & prove a blessing to your latter years, whilst I am always with true attachment my dear Friend your ever affectionate servant

J. Milne".

James had first met John Milne in Bussorah (Basra) when pioneering the overland route for despatches in 1802. Under cover of being a doctor, he was an influential part of the Government intelligence organisation.

In contrast to the lengthy letters penned by his friend, his brother George's were brief, usually ending with –

"......I have written the usual "Bill of Health" for his Reverence at Abernethy. Wishing your Lady and Self many happy days, I remain your most Affectionate Brother

Geo Grant".

He made no mention of his personal life. James was concerned that George's health was not as good as he would have his father believe. Parson John seemed resigned to the fact that he probably would not live to see him return from India. He was accordingly more appreciative of James's frequent visits to Abernethy and assistance with business matters.

He was surprised that Donald Mackintosh was taking so long to wind up the Colonel's affairs. James and himself had been nominated executors of his neighbour Major Charles Grant of Auchernack's estate which, despite complications over an illegitimate daughter, they had expeditiously dealt with. He conceded that it may have been difficult having to correspond from a distance with fellow executors situated far from Edinburgh.

Donald's fellow executors were; the Colonel's widow in Nairn, William Mackintosh of Balnespick the Colonel's nephew in Kincraig, and Sir Aeneas Mackintosh of Mackintosh. The Mackintosh's sister was married to William Balnespick's late father, Elizabeth's uncle. Sir Aeneas and Lady Mackintosh came to stay at Viewfield in September 1818.

Lady Mackintosh wrote to Elizabeth from Aberdeen –

"My dear Madam
Mr Grant and you may think we have been lost -
However we are thus far on our return home. I shall
refer all particulars till we have the pleasure of
seeing you both at Nairn. We have passed two days
with my sister and niece here &, God willing, are to
set out tomorrow morning for Nairn, where if you
and Mr Grant are at home and dear children in
health we propose sleeping at your house and calling
on your Mother and Mr & Mrs Mackintosh on
Monday. As we are not sure of post horses I cannot
say at what Hour but think about tea time on Sunday
ye 6th. I am going to write for our own servant and
horses to come down to meet us that we may get
home the short way. The ladies desire to join with Sir
Aeneas and me in affectionate Compliments etc
                    Margaret Mackintosh.
PS Should you see our Geddes friends pray remember
us most kindly to them both".

Sir Aeneas wrote to James on 1st October 1818 from Moyhall –

"My dear Sir
I have been favored with your letters of the 20th, 22
and 23rd ult by which Lady Mackintosh and I are
extremely concerned to learn that the indisposition of
our amiable friend Mrs Grant was the cause of our
being deprived of her and your agreeable Society
when the Raigmores (recently married) *were here,*
but I hope by return of the Bearer that you will be
able to give us favorable account of your Invalid.

Lady Mackintosh has been complaining of late but is now better. Mrs Mackintosh (Raigmore) seems to be an agreeable young woman and desirous to please. She sings and plays well, and they appear to be happy.

Even in this high country our crops are a month earlier than former years, for at this time last year we only began to cut. Now we have got 2/3 of it in the stackyard. Bear is an excellent heavy crop, Oats thin but good grain. The Potatoes are larger but not so numerous as last year. The Cattle, Sheep and Wool sold well. In short we have two succeeding years equally good. The Highlanders will in a great measure forget their distresses and Proprietors will get some rent. We are glad that worthy Mrs Grant has at last thought of Forres. I am sure her daughter would prefer London.

For a considerable time past we have intended a visit to Rossshire, but something or other came in our way to prevent the accomplishment. God willing, if Lady Mackintosh be strong enough to undertake the excursion, we shall set out upon it next week, and when we get home, shall have the pleasure to write to you.

The Person who delivers this will carry home the cask of herring which you was so kind as to procure for us and, to pay for which, I enclose two Pound notes. The balance you will please give to the bearer. Yours etc

PS I regret there are only two Muirfowl in the House. All hands being so busy at the harvest, we are loath to send in quest of them".

The Viewfield and Millbank harvests were gathered in long before those in the mountains of Moy. The indigenous Grouse or Muirfowl had been plentiful for a season or two. Only a few of Henry Shank's "Petericks" or Partridges were to be found amidst the turnips of the low ground.

The affairs of Forres were of concern to Colonel Francis who wrote from Cullen House on the 16th of September 1819 –

> *"Dear Sir*
> *I have to return you my best thanks for your letter of yesterday with which I am just now favored replying. Mr M's resignation of the office of Dean of Guild, is an event which after the disagreement of last year need not be much regretted by his Brethren. The vacancy occasioned by the death of our excellent friend Burdyard although much more to be lamented than the other, will certainly as you observe be far easier to supply. I have asked Mr Alex Grant at Bradhill to become a Councillor in the room of our late friend and I would fain hope he would consent, but like you I find some difficulty as to a proper person to succeed the present Dean of Guild because the situation should or rather I suspect must be held by a resident trading Burgess and unquestionably it is desirable that he should be a man both of discretion and respectability. Were it not very inconvenient for you I would entreat your taking the trouble of having a personal conference on the subject with Baillie Mitchell who perhaps may be able to suggest some fit person and should there be any great difficulty in prevailing on the gentleman suggested to accept, you wd find the parson of Forres a most useful auxilliary*

in reasoning with him - at all events I will trust to your writing Mr Mitchell about it.

Probably Friday the 24th for the previous Meeting and Monday the 27th for the Election may be as proper days as can be chosen for the business & if you think so, it will be obliging to cause it to be notified, but any days will answer, care only being taken to have at least 48 Hours between them and to have the Election over on or before the 29th. Yrs etc.

Colonel Francis held the patronage of the Burgh of Forres and with James, the current Provost, could decide for the most part who should be on the Town Council, a situation which prevailed until the Reforms of 1832.

In October 1819 James's local standing was further enhanced by his appointment as Deputy Lieutenant of Nairnshire.

The Lord Lieut of Nairnshire James Brodie of Brodie wrote –

"Sir
I feel much gratified in having to communicate, in consequence of a letter from Lord Sidmouth of the 7th Inst, that His Royal Highness the Prince Regent has approved of you as a Depute Lieut for Nairnshire".

Confirmation was supplied by his Deputy, Col Rose of Kilravock –

"Sir
By desire of Mr Brodie of Brodie, His Majesty's Lieutenant for the County of Nairn, I beg leave to acquaint you that your Commission as a Deputy Lieutenant of that County lies with Mr Murray Writer in Nairn.

I have the honour to be Sir Your most obedient humble servant

Hugh Rose, Vice Lieut Nairnshire".

Parson John congratulated his son on the honour conferred on him, and wrote on the 1st of January 1820 –

"My dear James
This being the first letter I have attempted this morning, my mind is so full of Ideas that I am not able to collect them, but in general to direct our hearts wishes to God for having given us such a son & that we are alive to see & understand the conduct of providence in making you the instrument of so much good to us, & giving you the heart and ability: I will stop as I hope you understand what is within us without my word. We are as when I wrote you last as to health, & now that I am 81, I wish for some time past to express my desire & hope that if it please God to keep us here till another summer that you, Mrs Grant, Johnnie & etc will come up and pass some short time with us in this place, where I have been for 55 years & while my eyes are open to see the children of our beloved son. Your Mother is by me just now & joins Your Affectionate Father

John Grant".

He had difficulty in remembering all his grandchildren's names. "Etc" covered Eliza, Christina and Augusta. The latter was born on the 14th of October 1819. Sadly he did not see them. He died on the 20th of January 1820, the same day as Sir Aeneas Mackintosh of Mackintosh.

15. The Death of Parson John

Parson John was laid to rest in the family plot at Duthil. James's immediate concern was the welfare of his mother. He stayed at the Manse until his sister was able to relieve him.

Helen's husband Alex Grant had received a letter of condolence from Edinburgh from his employer, J.P.Grant of Rothiemurchus –

"I need not tell you with what regret all this family learnt the loss you have sustained in the death of our excellent & respected Minister of Abernethy. You know there was no person remaining in the Country for whom I had so great a feeling of attachment, or whom I looked on as so useful a member of our little Society - and I can assure you that this feeling was sincerely partaken by all of us from the youngest to the oldest. Pray convey to Mrs Grant & to your mother-in-law the expression of our sympathy in their affliction. It is a great consolation to those who have survived him to know that there is nothing connected to his memory which does not reflect credit on those who were related to him, that he lived happy from the excellent temper & disposition of his mind, communicating a portion of his own cheerfulness to all who enjoyed the pleasure of his society, & diffusing to the utmost extent of his influence all the more substantial benefits which his good advice & the exertion of his active benevolence could bestow. Believe me Sir yours with great regard J P Grant".

His daughter Elizabeth was to mention Parson John in her "Memoirs of a Highland Lady".

A close friend of the family Major Dan Mitchell, who had married Charles Forbes's sister, wrote from 9 Fitzroy Square in London –

"My dear Grant
The intimation of the death of your lamented father only reached me yesterday. It awakened in my mind many a tender recollection. To the departed I was early in life deeply indebted for many kind offices and for an exertion of Friendship which I hope never to forget. Forsaken by my own father I found in yours, a zeal, a benevolence and a warmth of heart; which I have not seen surpassed by any subsequent friend whom it pleased providence to bless me with. To you who so well knew his worth, any panegyric of mine, is indeed out of place; and yet I cannot refrain from saying that I have never known a man of a more candid nature or who had in his composition more of the fine feelings of a gentleman; and all these qualities were grafted upon an honest & kind heart and on an independent and manly mind. I entreat of you to assure your affectionate and kind hearted mother that Mrs Mitchell and I most sincerely condole with her on her irreparable loss - and I assure you we unfeignedly sympathise with your sister and you on this melancholy event".

Alexander Walker wrote –

"We have been from home for some weeks which has prevented me from answering your letter announcing the loss of your excellent and worthy

144

Parent. I most sincerely condole and sympathise with you in this loss. At whatever period and age this happens it is an event that we must always deplore. Your good Father has left the World in the maturity of years and in the height of a reputation acquired by the exercise of virtue and benevolence. I do not know of any life more productive of happiness and respect than that of a reasonable clergyman who has a disposition to do good. The affections of a parent never can be extinguished. Nothing would be more pure and delightful to your Father than your return from India and the enjoyment which you have since had of his society would be a mutual source of pleasure unalloyed by any unhallowed mixture. I speak on this subject from experience, as the short time that my own venerable and excellent Mother survived after my arrival in this Country was I believe one of the happiest periods of human existence. It was an advantage my dear Grant to be reared and educated by such parents for which I can never sufficiently express my gratitude. Neither reason nor revelation forbid us to believe that they are still anxious for our welfare and I confess that this idea is pleasant and agreeable".

There were many more letters of condolence.

The congregation asked James to approve a memorial to their Minister which they wished to install in the church –

"Sacred to the memory of the Reverend John Grant, Minister of Abernethy, who departed this life on the 21st day of January in the year of Our Lord 1820 at the advanced age of eighty one years - deeply lamented by his beloved parishioners, who, with

grateful sense of the exemplary fidelity, with which he watched for their souls during the long period of fifty six years, and of his unwearied zeal for their happiness and prosperity, consecrate this last mournful tribute to the piety and virtues of their revered guide and benefactor".

Another Minister would in due course replace him and the Manse would have to be vacated. James set about arranging a roup. Alex Grant a licenced auctioneer from Grantown organised the sale which took place on the 23rd and 24th of May. He was assisted by William Duffus who acted as Clerk. The household effects and farm stock were sold on the two days in May. The crops on the Glebe and on land at Upper Dell rented from the Seafield Estates were to be sold on the 4th and 6th of October.

In the May sales there were 748 separate lots which realised £822.12s.5d. Some lots were described as "Trock" or collections of small wares. They realised anything from, 1d for old iron, to £34.10/- for a pair of draught oxen. For £26 the Minister of Cromdale bought Parson John's gig. 42 blankets were sold individually for an average of 15/- (75p in today's money). The livestock included 32 Cattle and 120 sheep.

A copy of the Roup Roll containing 26 pages lists details of each lot and gives the name and residence of the purchaser and the sale price. It is possible to visualise how the sale proceeded and who was bidding against whom. There were 188 different purchasers from as far afield as Badenoch, Strathdon and Forres. Those who paid in cash received a discount of 5%. The remainder provided Bills falling due at a later date.

The Judge of the Roup was Capt McGregor of Delavorar in the upper reaches of Strathavon. Capt Grant of Congash opposite Grantown, on the Spey, who was the local factor for Seafield estates, assisted James in banking the cash and in collecting individual "Bills" when they fell due. The money was banked on behalf of James's mother with the British Linen Bank, Forres, whose Manager was Mr Cumming.

Before the sale in May James's Mother went to stay with her Ballintomb cousins at Craggan near Grantown, and afterwards to her daughter Helen's at Garmouth. As the widow of a Minister of the Church of Scotland she was entitled to a pension, which James organised with Sir Henry Moncrieff, Treasurer of the Widows' Fund.

James notified Donald Stoddart, 9 Carlton Chambers, Regent Street, London of his father's death. He was the agent for receiving his half pay as Chaplain to the 97th Regiment, and was asked to advise how his mother should apply for a pension. Parson John was commissioned on the 8th of

February 1794. Stoddart expressed his sympathies and wrote –

"Your mother is clearly entitled to the pension of £30 per annum. There was a small sum due to her husband from 25th December to the date of his death".

There was evidently some difficulty in establishing his widow's right to an army pension. Her appeal was refused, so James asked Colonel Francis as an MP to take the matter up with the authorities. He received a reply from Lord Palmerston at the War Office –

"I have to acknowledge the receipt of your letter of the 5th Ultimo, enclosing a memorial from the Widow of the late John Grant Chaplain on half pay of the 97th Foot, and to acquaint you that I am sorry that I cannot see sufficient grounds for recommending an alteration in the decision already communicated to her on the subject of her claim to the Pension.

I have the honor to be Sir Your most obedient humble servant

Palmerston".

As the season progressed, Capt Grant of Congash suggested the October dates for the Corn Roup should be the 4th at the Manse and the 6th at the Dell to avoid clashing with the Grantown Cattle Tryst. People would be reluctant to buy green corn at an earlier date for fear of its being later frosted. The sale realised £286.4s.

Parson John had acted as banker for a number of his parishioners, holding money on their behalf with the bank in Forres, and paying them interest. These "Obligations" had to be repaid. There were the usual outstanding accounts to be paid to merchants in Grantown and Abernethy, to the shoemaker, smith and carpenter, to John Allan for caring for the crops etc. etc.

A few people were tardy in honouring the bills granted at the time of the roups when they became due. They were pursued in the courts by Mr James Philips, Writer in Nairn. It took two years finally to wind up Parson John's estate which was valued at a net sum of £113.10s, all of which was due to his widow and forwarded to Alex Grant at Garmouth where she was staying. Alex wrote on the 13th March 1823 –

"My Dear James - Your letter of the 11th Inst I had the pleasure of receiving enclosing accounts of disbursements with the affairs at Abernethy which certainly have been wound up in a most accurate manner, and strange to say without a shilling of loss. I have also received your draft on London for £113.10/-, the balance remaining after all claims against the estate have been liquidated. On the interest account, if calculated, the balance would have been decidedly due to yourself. (He refers to a letter of 9th and offer of £100 from James). Regarding the appropriation of the balance of the Abernethy money I have only to say that your disinterested liberality to me upon this as well as on

many other occasions is beyond what I have words to express.

I shall out of the £113.10/- add as much to the India money as will make up £850 and deposit it in the hands of Col Grant as you suggest... I shall give it to Mr Brander for it to be added to the sums formerly deposited in his hands in your mothers name.

It is probable it will not be taken at Cullen until Colonel Grant returns from London.

The weather has continued so unfavourable that we have not as yet been able to get down any timber which retards the relief in anticipation - but the time is now close at hand when it must come, and the near prospect gives me additional confidence and expectation. After this we shall have monthly supplies of money which will be gradually diminishing my Engagements until the whole is liquidated".

The India money came from the estate of James's brother George. In a business letter to Capt Grant of Congash dated 31st May 1820 James wrote –

"My mother whom I've left at Garmouth thanks you for your help. Just heard my brother George died last Dec. He was a Capt in the Bombay army & adjutant & quartermaster general to the subsidiary force in Gujerat".

George had died on 19th December 1819, a month before his father.

16. Brother George's Children

It was merciful that Parson John did not live to learn of his son's death. He would have found it difficult to reconcile himself to the fact that George had a family out of wedlock and by an Indian lady too, and had never told him. He was spared any grief by the fact that it was not until the 29th of May that news came of his passing.

James received a letter from Frank Warden in Bombay dated 6 Jan –

> *"My dear Grant*
> *Sorry to break such a long silence with news of your brother George's unexpected death. He was Asst QM General to the force at Baroda & held in the highest esteem in his profession. Will help if I can.*
>
> *Am to be married again. Knowing my steady judgment you will be aware that I am not throwing myself away.*
>
> *After 9 months taste of a Coucillor I have returned to the dear old Office under our friend Elphinstone. I trust the Hon'ble Court will, out of an act of justice to its functionaries, place my office on a par with our brethren at the sister Presidencies, Madras at least. Have memorialised the scandalous pay of my Secretaries. If any of my Hon'ble employers are within your reach I wish you would talk to them about this. Money should exert himself. I haven't had the chance to show attention to Mr Gordon, but no recommendation of yours shall ever go unnoticed.*

Shank & I have parted company. He is now keeping house with Meek. Bell & Prendergast quite well. There has been a sad disposition in your old Court of Circuit and Appeal.

The Jousmee Pirates are being suppressed.

Do you yet dispense justice as a Magistrate or are you turned farmer? Walker I hear has had an offer of a situation in Leadenhall Street.

God bless you my dear Friend etc

F Warden".

A more detailed account of events followed from Michie Forbes who was by now in charge of the Bombay office of Forbes & Co and wrote to George's mother. James prepared a resume of the contents of his letter dated 16th January 1820, received 6th June following, and the steps he took as a result –

"Intimated my Brother George's death at Baroda on 19th Decr 1819 - and the receipt from Capt Rose 2d Regt of Cavalry of copy of his Will dated 22 March 1817 - Capt Rose the sole Executor - the other two, Major Tundy & Lieutenant Pallinser being dead. Principal balance in the hands of Messrs Forbes & Co stated at Rs 17000 odd up to 16th Jany 1820.

Enclosure from Capt Rose dated 2d Jan 1820 with copy of the will by which 10,000 Rs are left to a native woman named Goolaut and three boys & a girl her children. Another child expected & unfortunately unprovided for. The 10,000 Rupees left to the Mother and Children born at the time of his death share and share alike - or to the survivor or survivors of them, and to be divided when the Youngest of the Children shall have attained the age of 14. Failing the children, the Mother to have the whole of that sum. All other Monies and property left to his Father and Mother for their use for ever - and failing either being alive at the time of his decease - then to his sister Helen & her heirs for ever. In aid of the limited allowance for the Children, Capt Rose to endeavour, through the interest of Mr Michie Forbes & other friends to get them admitted into the Bombay Charity School.

Wrote in consequence fully on 5th August 1820 to Mr Michie Forbes, Capt Rose and Mr Warden, earnestly soliciting their good offices to the family of the deceased - and mentioning that my Mother had authorized Messrs Forbes & Co of Bombay to retain 2,000 Rupees as a provision for the posthumous child. A debt of 6,000 Rs due to me by my brother for advances to him while I remained in India at the same time cancelled.

J A G".

Alexander Walker wrote from Bowland on the 17th June 1820 –

"I would ere now have answered your kind letter of the 31st but I have been prevented by engagements and a constant state of hurry. Col Fowler of the Madras Cavalry and Capt J Brown of our establishment only left me yesterday. The latter was a particular friend of your poor Brothers and spoke of him with great regret and regard. He was beloved by the officers and from his general behaviour as well as his professional character had acquired the esteem

and respect of the Service. The merits of our deceased friends condole us for their loss while they aggravate the misfortune. I sympathise with you my dear Grant on this painful occasion and it is perhaps fortunate that your venerable Father has been saved from this afflicting intelligence.

Warden has married I understand a Miss Kensington a daughter of a banker of that name who failed some years ago in London. He deserves a good wife and would even make a convert of a bad one. They are all delighted with their new Governor, and altho this is always the case at first with every change, I believe they have every reason to indulge the highest expectation from Mr Elphinstone. He has begun by increasing the Army which is always a popular measure. The Artillery have received an addition of one Battn and two more Regts of Cavalry are proposed to be raised. A third Member of the Medical Board has been recommended. Carnac has come home and I expect him down here before the summer closes. He was compelled to this step by bad health both of himself and his wife. Williams will of course succeed at Baroda. Shank I understand is on his way to this Country and Crozier has come home to solicit that appointment to which he has certaintly served a very long apprenticeship. But you will have heard of all this before".

Aunt Foster replied to James's letter informing her of George's death, from Paris –

"My dear Augustus
Your kind letter of the 28th Octr did indeed interrupt the happiness we had been enjoying for some little time; so mixed are all the events of this transitory

existence, it was the more painful to support, never having before heard, that your Brother George had been much inconvenienced by that abominable climate; sincerely do we all sympathize with you and your Mother in this additional trial - how fortunate for her you are returned and settled so near her.

I do not know if you had any communications with young Wilberforce Bird who was in the Benares Station - we have just heard of his decease in the prime of life and high reputation.

It is with much pleasure I can thank you for all your kind wishes towards your cousin Mary. She is quite well and safe arrived at Florence, where her husband tells Foster in a letter received the other day she is universally a favorite with all the Friends he has introduced her to. They have a very respectable and select society of English there. His letter was dated the 22d Ult when he said it was as mild as May. When they arrived it was very cold. Our weather here has been something of the same description - on the shortest day we walked in the Bois de Boulogne and found it most delightful - it began freezing on the 24th and for several days was 10 degrees below freezing point. Friday it began to thaw and now is quite pleasant.

All your friends here are well and unite with me in wishing you and all dear to you many happy returning years. Foster's eldest boy is gone to school altogether but comes home every other Sunday, being situated very near us. The second goes to the "Ensignment Mutuette" from half past 8 to 4 or 5 where he is getting on. They have all had the whooping cough this Autumn & Winter but are recovered.

155

I remain my dear Nephew your most affectionate
Aunt Grant".

The interrupted happiness to which she referred, was the wedding of her daughter Mary, about which she wrote to James from Paris on the 19th of October 1820 –

> *"My dear Augustus*
> *I cannot suffer the papers to inform you of an event that has taken place in my Family this morning. Your cousin Mary was married at the Ambassador's Chapel to Mr Charles Thelluson, cousin of Ld Rendlesham who is living in Florence with his family, where they are to join them. The journey will be very pleasing as the weather will be getting milder as they proceed. I have only time to add that Mr James Wilkinson & his wife are now living near us. He is a most agreeable pleasant Man but a martyr to the gout.*
>
> *Accept our united best love to you and Yours and have the goodness to inform the rest of our friends of this event which I trust will be productive of much happiness - believe me*
> *Your Affectionate*
> *Aunt Grant."*

Although James's mother was solicitous for her newly disclosed grandchildren and was making practical provision for the one yet unborn, she particularly requested that no one should write to her about the "India Business" when Alex took her to stay for a few weeks with the Ballintombs at

Craggan. The happy union of her niece Mary contrasted somewhat with the revelation of the liaison formed by her son George.

The transfer of the balance of his estate to her was effected with the help of William Bridgman. Included was bullion in the form of a number of gold Mohins, which he suggested be sold immediately rather than waiting for a doubtful rise in their price. When James agreed he wrote –

> *"Instead of forwarding the enclosed direct to your good mother, I have thought it better to transmit it through you, that you may see something of the mysteries of Remittances in Gold, which however I think the ruling powers in India will soon put a stop to".*

Alex forwarded a Bill for £390.19.3 from Bridgman which James paid into an account with the British Linen Bank in Elgin in his mother's name, together with £383.16.2, the proceeds of the Mohuns. Alex was to make the total invested with the Bank up to £850 from the balance of Parson John's estate and retain the rest to cover his own and his mother-in-law's expenses. On Colonel Francis's return from Parliament the £850 was to be invested in a bond with Seafield Estates.

At that time in October 1822 it was not clear whether James's mother would remain at Craggan or return from Strathspey to Viewfield or to

Garmouth. Alex said that the joists of his new cottage were ready for the roof.

In June he had sent James a plan of the house which he proposed to build, and an explanation of the circumstances –

"In the outsett of negotiations with my local Laird, I had frequently said that rather than pay an extravagant price for accommodation, I would build a small cottage for myself. This I certainly had no serious intention of doing at first, nor did he (my Laird) consider I was serious, but thought as there was no other house in the village that would answer as a point of room, that I should in the end be obliged to come into his terms. Rothiemurchus however, hearing of our negotiations, wrote me a very handsome letter in which he offered to make me a present in the meantime of timber to build me a house, which house he said if I should leave Garmouth he would take off my hands at a valuation. I still made use of this letter, without any intention of building, in the hope it might bring my Laird to more reasonable terms, but he persisted in his former terms - and then, and not till then, I formed the serious resolution of doing something in the way of building - somewhat reluctantly I do assure you. But to make a long story short I have now contracted for a cottage, agreeable to a plan and specification which I send you herewith for your perusal & which I doubt not you will consider very cheap accommodation at a very moderate cost i.e.

Price contracted for	*£250.00/-*
Slates delivered to the ground	*£20.00/-*
All actual outlays for the stones may be	*£50.00/-*
Copper, slate nails -	*£3.10/-*
	£323.10/-

This will cover to the full all my outlay for the house and allowing £100 for making a garden and some small accommodation for a couple of cows and my horse I shall have my whole Villa under £450.

The next and principal point upon which you will naturally wish to expect to receive information is, whether I am prepared with money for this undertaking - and I have pleasure in saying that I have nearly the sum required as a Balance in my own favor in my cash with the Business which I can lay my hands on at any time. I am free of debt of any kind, and my little shipping property is now perfectly clear and unencumbered. Excepting some trifling accounts the whole of which will not amount to £40, I am entirely free of debt. I hope therefore that all whose opinions I respect and who wish me well, will not look upon my plan in any way imprudent. Were I to quit Rothy's Business tomorrow I know not where I could reside more retired or more economically than where I am, and while I have shipping property, my residence must necessarily be by the Seaside and this place is as favourable a situation as any other.

I hope to commence building in three or four weeks, to have it roofed in and the first coat of plaster on before the winter and to have it completely finished by the first of April.

The greater part of the stones I shall have on the ground by the end of next week. I get them down from Lossiemouth as ballast of vessels free of freight and my own horse carts them from the shore. The cost of the stones at Lossiemouth is 21d per ton".

Once built, the house would provide sufficient accommodation for his family and Helen's mother, who was insisting on paying her share of expenses, since George had made her such a generous bequest.

They learned more about his children when his executor Capt Rose visited Nairn. He had written in August 1823 to say that he & Capt Elder of the Bombay European Regt, whom Mr Grant might recollect at Broach, were visiting Col Mair at Fort George and staying a week at Bennet's Hotel Inverness and would call if James was at home. He and Elder were to return to Bombay in Dec or Jan next. They were invited to stay at Viewfield. Capt Rose, before leaving Bombay in November 1821, had settled the girl and two boys at school at 10Rs each per month leaving the eldest boy & young child with the mother. The youngest child had since died and the R2,000 reserved for him reverted to Parson John's widow.

Following Capt Rose's visit James wrote to Francis Warden, Chief Sec to Gov of Bombay on 6Dec 1823

Although from distance and other causes our intercourse is often interrupted, you will, I am sure, readily believe, that I can never feel indifferent to your welfare, or cease to bear in remembrance the many happy days I spent in your Society. I wrote to you formerly respecting my poor brother's unfortunate family, and I now trouble you again at the instance of his executor Captain Rose, who has been unremitting in his good offices to them. Captain Rose has been in this Country on furlough and returns to India by one of the China ships. I learn from him that it would be desirable to get one of the boys, who is dark, into the Guicwar's service on the footing of Selledhar, and that the accomplishment of this object would be facilitated, if not ensured, by a few lines from you to Mr Williams, the Resident at Baroda. Pray therefore do the needful and you will greatly oblige me. The other two boys are at school at Bombay, and Captain Rose thinks they cannot be better disposed of than by being made sub- assistant Surgeons, a new order introduced into the medical line since I left India. I have written to Philipps on this subject, and should any difficulty arise which your influence can remove, I know your assistance will not be withheld. I am so sensible of Captain Rose's attention to these poor helpless objects that I would regard any little countenance or kindness you may be so good as to shew him as a favor conferred upon myself".

James noted - Communication to the same effect made under the same date to Benjamin Philipps Esq, 1st Member of the Medical Board at Bombay - and to Capt Rose, then on the eve of departure for India.

Francis Warden replied –

"I wrote to Williams immediately on receipt of your letter and he replied,"I have been favored with your note inclosed respecting Captain Grant's child and will be very happy to exert myself for him. You must let me know his age and where he is to be found. I shall be able to get him into the service with a line or two in the first instance, and will push him forward as occasion may offer.

On applying to Captain Rose for information of these particulars, I find that they (the other two boys) are both at an excellent institution, the Charity School in Bombay, whence it will be a pity to remove them until they finish what is taught there. The Boys are well looked after and the "under" situations in the medical line & other branches of the service are open to them. You may depend upon it I will not lose sight of Your wishes in respect of them.

I must now my dear friend bid you adieu. Years have silvered my locks but they have effected no change in the sincerity of disposition with which I have ever been & am yours affectionately

F Warden".

17. Beauchamp's Daughter Nona

Whilst dealing with his brother's offspring, a similar situation arose concerning his brother-in-law Beauchamp Mackintosh. He wrote regularly to Elizabeth expressing his frustration at the slow progress up the ladder of promotion. He had been involved in the Deccan campaign in central India and was feeling run down. He died on the 31st of January 1822.

Elizabeth learned of the event from her cousin William Mackintosh of Geddes who was in Edinburgh on business. He had received a letter there on the 9th of July from Beauchamp's Commanding Officer, Lt Colonel William Munro. All officers on active service were encouraged to draw up their wills. It was easy to ascertain his wishes. He had nominated "Geddes" and Col Munro, together with Major Caddell and Major J J Mackintosh of Farr, as his executors.

Elizabeth was surprised to learn that her brother had a daughter by an Indian woman. He left £3,000 to be held in Trust for the girl, to be used for her education, board and lodging and expenses. Once she was twenty one and independent of her guardians the interest would be hers and the capital reserved for her issue, thus safeguarding her fortune from a future husband. Beauchamp made some small bequests, including one to John

Storm in Calcutta. The balance of his estate was to be divided equally between his surviving brothers and sisters.

John Storm when thanking James for helping his brother William wrote –

> *"I come now to a most painful subject. I come to condole with the family of my dearest friend Beauchamp, who has been cut off in the prime of life, and within a brief period of that happy meeting which he had anticipated as near at hand with the most ardent feelings - poor fellow, the recurring hopes of such a meeting served to gladden many hours of his many years of servitude. (He had been due to return home). His relations must ever mourn his early fate - his acquaintances will ever revere his memory. His accomplishments, the virtue of a Man and a Soldier which he possessed, combined with the rare benevolence of his heart, endeared him to every acquaintance and to none more so than myself. Will you my dear Sir convey my sincere condolences to his family on this mournful occasion. I have been absent from Calcutta for nearly two months, otherwise I should have addressed Mrs Mackintosh or William. At the distance of time I feel unwilling to open a wound yet so fresh. To them and to your Lady I beg to be mentioned with respect and affection; and to request of her to offer my sympathizing condolence to Mrs MacDonald".*

Beauchamp's daughter had been born in 1817. She was residing with Mr Conductor Dewsnap's family in Madras. The executors had had her christened Margaret Nona. Major Mackintosh Farr was returning home and it was suggested that he accompany Nona to Scotland where it was hoped that her Uncle William would take care of her.

William and his wife Jane Galloway had no children. He thought his niece might help his wife at Millbank. His sister Margaret Macdonald pointed out that as she was only six, his expectations were unrealistic.

Her £3,000 fortune was invested in a Trust to be administered by Maj Mackintosh of Farr, Geddes and James Augustus Grant. William was happy to provide accommodation for his niece at Millbank, paid for out of the interest from trust funds. In fact this development came at an opportune moment as he had overreached himself and was pinched for cash. He lost no time in pointing out to Donald Mackintosh, who controlled his mother's trust, that his expectations when she died would be one quarter of his mother's money instead of a fifth. Surely Donald would now lend him more of his mothers trust funds in consequence. He and his sisters Elizabeth and Margaret together with Guyon each received over £1500 from their brother's estate.

Nona arrived in Nairn in July 1823. It was quite a daunting four month journey for her, to relations whom she had never met. She was six, the same age as Christina. James's daughters were intrigued by their cousin's colouring and beautiful long dark hair. She soon became accepted as one of the family. It seemed easier for Beauchamp's daughter as a girl to be accepted in society than it would have been to introduce George's boys.

James and Elizabeth now had five daughters, Margaret Mary had been born on the 14th of April 1821 and Helen on the 24th of October 1822. The high proportion of girls in the family was commented on by Alexander Walker –

"I was much gratified a few days ago by the receipt of your letter of the 16th. It is always refreshing to me to receive a letter from you, tho it comes but seldom, and to see your well known writing. I often regret that we have not contrived sometimes to meet, if it were but to give our families the advantage of an early acquaintance and to have an opportunity ourselves of talking over old times.

Mrs Walker and I beg to offer to you and Mrs Grant our most cordial and sincere congratulations on the addition to your family. The safety of Mrs Grant makes this a double blessing; for notwithstanding the fortitude and resolution with which women support their pains it is a moment of anxiety and terror. Salute the young stranger for us and give her the blessing of a friend. It is perhaps lucky that you have so large a proportion of females. Their introduction into life will give you less uneasiness and there is less chance of losing their society entirely. I shall probably be as much at a loss to chuse a profession for my sons as I am now to chuse the best method of educating them. I told you in some former letter that I proposed to place them at a public school and that

Mrs Walker and I meant for a few years at least to keep them company. Many people will laugh at this plan and will even say that children should not be trained up by their parents. We are old fashioned enough to think differently and to imagine that instruction will be as faithfully and carefully communicated under the eye of a Mother and Father as under the sole direction of a stranger. But this is not the sole reason; our children are but infants and require our care while we shall enjoy the pleasure of their little society. They have already made some progress. The eldest is reading Caesar and the youngest has been once through the rudiments. We have not yet fixed on a school".

They did in fact decide on a school, in Durham, where they took a house. James reserved a special place for correspondence with his friend, which apparently lapsed after the year 1822. The last letter he preserved, which Alexander Walker wrote from Durham, explains the reason.

"My dear Grant
I should have written before this if I had had anything to say except about myself. You will have seen by the Papers that I have been appointed to St Helena and on the whole I am satisfied with what I have done. I hope and think that the appointment may contribute to the advantage and happiness of my family. It provides some employment for myself; It is an honourable situation and attended with some profit. But all this you will say is not a little fanciful when you recollect the miserable crib we slept in and the gladness with which we bade adieu, an eternal adieu as I then thought to that remote island. As far as I can see at present I am making as little sacrifice

as possible. Mrs Walker and the two boys accompany me. I shall carry a tutor out with me and I trust for four years at their time of life that their education may be prosecuted under this system with advantage. We shall not commence our voyage before August and perhaps it may be later. I am anxious to see the end of the present term at this school which finishes on the 20th of June, but it is possible that we shall be obliged to leave them and visit our friends in Scotland. All this will depend on the intelligence we receive of the sailing of a vessel for St Helena.

I saw Mrs Shank and her children. She is both a prudent and an affectionate Mother. Shank is expected to arrive in this Country in two or three months hence.

I fear there will be little chance of our meeting before we go. We shall be tied down by our arrangements and must pass a month at least in London before we sail; but I should be delighted to take you once more by the hand, to be introduced to Mrs Grant and your little group. I shall hope and trust however that all this will happen on some future day; but we must not be too curious about futurity. It was on Saturday last that I arrived from London and I am not yet recovered of the want of two nights rest and the jolting of the Coach. Mrs Walker joins in every kind wish to Mrs Grant and yourself and I ever remain my dear Grant with sincere regards. Yrs

A Walker".

After Napoleon's death in 1821, St Helena was handed back to the Company by the British Government.

1823 saw the end of another long running correspondence with James's Aunt Foster. She wrote from Paris on the 26th of October.

"My dear James Augustus.
I have long delayed writing to you on account of my continued indisposition since the beginning of the summer, hoping from month to month to tell you I was materially improved in Health; which I am sorry to say is not the case. I am now induced to employ an Amanuensis to inform you of a melancholy event which has taken place in our family which has plunged us all in the deepest affliction, in the sudden death of Mrs Foster Grant on friday the 24th instant.

I request you will inform Forbes and the rest of the family of the loss of My Daughter, as my son is too afflicted in this moment to write any letters we can spare him. Your Uncle and the rest of the family are well and I hope you will be able to send me a good account of all around you to whom we beg to be kindly remembered and I remain Your Affectionate
Aunt Grant".

James noted "Wrote to Strathdon & Garmouth 11Nov."

The following month he received a letter from her daughter Jane –

"My dear Cousin
It is with sentiments of the most poignant grief that I commence a correspondence to give you the melancholy information of the death of our

169

inestimable Mother, whom it has pleased the Almighty to release from her sufferings on the 5th instant. Our beloved parent had been lingering many months with a most painful disease, which she supported throughout with truly Christian patience and fortitude, and without ever uttering a complaint, the only consolation we can at the moment feel in our severe affliction is that her last hours were free from pain and she expired in her sleep surrounded by her weeping children of which blessing she was perfectly sensible to the last. My poor Mother received much gratification from your last kind letter, and my Brother begs me to offer you his warmest regards and that he will shortly address you himself.

We were glad to hear so good an account of Mrs Grant and your young family to whom My Sister and Myself entreat you will offer our affectionate remembrance and accept the same my dear Cousin from yours truly

Jane Grant".

James was saddened by the passing of his Aunt and the knowledge that he would no longer be entertained and heartened by her newsy letters. To her he owed the abbreviation of his name to JAG and his father's name "Parson John". He was known locally as "Pastor John", but this seemed to her not to describe his true character.

She saw him as an affable English country vicar to be met with in her native Norfolk. She liked calling James by his middle name Augustus. She insisted on calling his father "Parson John" to such an extent that he was thereafter known in the family by that name.

On the 23rd of July 1825, Elizabeth gave birth to a sixth daughter who was named Mary Foster in memory of her affectionate Aunt.

18. Death of Johnnie and birth of Jamesina

Viewfield was filled with the chatter of the seven young Grants. They were joined briefly by their Macdonald cousins. Ranald had died leaving Margaret with four boys under nine and little else.

James was a trustee of their marriage settlement and helped her to become established in Edinburgh where the children were assured of a good education. Margaret relied more on James than on his fellow trustee, Donald Mackintosh, which piqued the latter somewhat. He had invested her fortune in a bond with Lord Eskdale. The security was good but he had to be constantly reminded to pay the interest on time. James arranged for Margaret to transfer her money into a bond with Lord Seafield provided by his friend Colonel Francis.

Elizabeth made sure that the children did not disturb James in his study, whilst attending to business. At other times he was an approachable and affectionate father. He regularly "escaped" to Forres where for the second time he was elected Provost. It was decided to grant the Freedom of the Burgh to Sir James McGrigor.

As Doctor McGrigor, Sir James had been Wellington's Chief Medical Officer throughout the Peninsular campaign. There were many casualties and their efficient care played a part in maintaining morale. The Doctor organised prefabricated hospitals and used his initiative in evacuating the wounded. He was not afraid to state his case to the Duke and, after metaphorically crossing swords with him, became a close friend. On one occasion when kicked by a horse Wellington lent him his own carriage. He became known as "Mac". After the final victory he was knighted and promoted to be Director General of the Army Medical Board.

Sir James married one of the daughters of Grant of Findrassie near Elgin who was a distant cousin of James's. The granting of the freedom was described in the Gazette –

> The Provost, Magistrates and Town Council of Forres, availing themselves of the presence of Sir James McGrigor MD, Director General of the Medical Department of the British Army, unanimously voted to him on the 25th of September 1825 the Freedom of the Burgh, and the same was presented at a dinner given by the local authorities to that respected individual by the hands of the Provost J A Grant Esq of Viewfield.

The dinner took place on the 29th of that month, and the Provost addressed Sir James, on the occasion, in the following terms

> *"In the name of the Magistrates and Town Council, I have the honor of presenting to you the Freedom of the Town of Forres, and I beg to assure you, that I*

experience great personal satisfaction in conveying to you this testimony of their respect as eminently to your character, talents and Services; nor can I but add my warmest wishes for your health, happiness and prosperity."

Alexander Carmichael, who had introduced him to the workings of the Council when he first became a member, had died, leaving a widow, two sons and two daughters. James helped the eldest son, Ludovick at the start of his career in the city where William Bridgman found him employment. Calling on the good offices of his friend George Cumming, the local MP, James obtained a cadetship in the Company's army in Madras for the younger son Robert.

Following the Union of the Parliaments in 1707, each county in Scotland returned one member except a few smaller ones, which were paired, each alternately sending a representative. Nairnshire was linked to Cromarty and took it in turns to elect an MP. Cumming had been recently elected.

The four "Western Boroughs" of Inverness, Nairn, Forres and Fortrose formed one constituency. Each sent a delegate to the election forum who cast votes for the candidates as agreed by their local electors. James was the delegate for Forres on two occasions.

The right to vote in the county and borough constituencies was limited to freeholders and persons with a substantial rental. Moves were afoot to extend the franchise and revise the constituencies, but for the time being the choice of MPs was in the hands of a few influential people. A similar situation prevailed in the Town or Burgh Councils.

James's brother-in-law William "Millbank" was involved with his friend Doctor Peter Macarthur in a dispute with Nairn Town Council over the sale of land at Mosshall. The individual members of the Council were each served with a writ to appear at the Baron's Court in Edinburgh. They were issued with a summons by a Messenger at Arms – John Wilson – witnessed by James Wilson and William Storm both indwellers in Nairn. The Town Council of Nairn was –

PROVOST
Sir William Gordon-Cumming of Gordonston and Altyre, Baronet

BAILLIES
William Robertson of Househill
John Ore residing in Nairn
Roderick Mackenzie residing in Nairn

DEAN OF GUILD
Alexander Macbeath merchant Nairn

TREASURER
James Philips Writer Nairn

COUNCILLORS

Charles Lennox Cumming Bruce of Roseisle & Kinnaird

The Hon Colonel Francis William Grant MP

Sir Archibald Dunbar of Northfield Baronet

Maj Gen William Grant of Tannachie

Lewis Dunbar Brodie of Burgie and Lethen

James Augustus Grant of Viewfield

Dr James Coull of Ashgrove

John Cumming Banker in Forres

Francis Smith of Waterford

Donald Smith Collector of Customs Inverness

Alexander Sutherland residing at Rose Valley

Captain James Rose residing in Nairn

Apart from James, the Bailies, Treasurer and Captain Rose, none of the other members, who included Colonel Francis, were residents of Nairn Burgh. Francis Smith was resident in Ireland! It was not surprising that reforms were thought to be necessary. James himself supported the status quo, believing, that provided the members were enlightened and conscientious, the method of appointing them produced the most efficient administration. Who knew what extreme radical might gain control of local affairs if the system was altered. As enlightened members, with the general interests of the population at heart, he trusted that his fellow Councillors would act altruistically.

In the summer of 1826 James returned from Forres one evening to find his son seriously ill. He immediately sent for Dr Robertson of Inverness to attend him. There was nothing he could do and young Johnnie died on the day before his twelfth birthday.

James later wrote to the Doctor -

"My dear Sir
From our recent and very heavy family affliction, added to a severe attack of rheumatism I have till within the last day or two been disqualified from holding a pen; and I can now but inadequately express my acknowledgements for the kindness of your professional visit on an occasion very interesting to Mrs Grant and myself. However painful the result, it was consolatory to us to have your presence and advice, and we shall always feel grateful for the promptitude with which you answered our call, and for the desire which you evinced to be serviceable on that occasion. As some return allow me to request your acceptance of the amount enclosed (£7) and to add that I remain etc."

Doctor Robertson replied –

"My dear Sir
The dispensation with which Providence has so recently visited your Family is indeed a sore one. If experience of similar afflictions enables us to sympathise in the sufferings of others, I am well qualified to participate in yours.

I have received your kind favor of yesterday's date & I thank you for its inclosure, greatly more than an ample remuneration for my visit which could not alas be of any use. Yrs etc."

James and Elizabeth received many expressions of sympathy on the loss of their only son. The older girls took a long time to get used to his absence. The fact that James had no male heir was of no importance to him. Elizabeth would have liked to have presented him with more boys. They had one more child born on the anniversary of Johnnie's death on the 5th of June 1827. It was another girl who they called Jamesina. It was common in those days to add "ina" to a boys name. Some sounded quite acceptable. Others such as Roderickina were a lifelong imposition on the recipient. The new arrival was soon called "Jemmy" by her sisters. Her future husband was to call her "Zena".

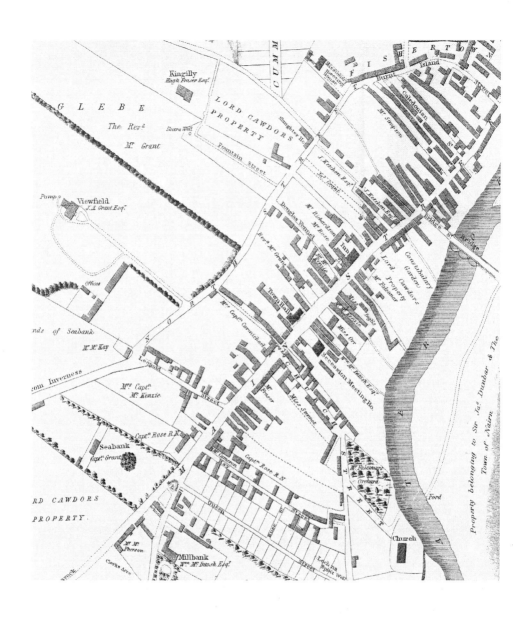

Figure 8 – Wood's 1821 Map of Nairn

179

19. Mrs Colonel Mackintosh's Trust

Shortly after Johnnie's death James learned of William Millbank's serious financial difficulties in a letter dated 5 Sep 1826.

"My Dear Sir
I am about to trouble you with some matters which I have repeatedly wished, particularly for the last few months, to consult you regarding.

When I came first to this quarter to reside, I was deeply encumbered with Glasgow Debts, and it took me a great length of time before I was enabled to get them arranged. Since then I have as you know made very large additions to my property in this Quarter and I have the satisfaction to believe, generally with prudence and advantage. I have however at same time got myself involved with different persons which added to the above cause has deeply involved me. Had the money market continued as it was some time back, I have reason to believe I would not have had to trouble you on the subject, but recent changes have made it impossible for me to carry through, without making sales, and this for many causes, I was unable to effect.

You and your family are my nearest relations, and as such, but entitled to succeed to such property as I may die possessed of, and consequently I consider myself as called on, to lay my circumstances fully and candidly before you, in order to obtain the benefit of your advice and assistance.

My Debts as per annexed List (No1) amount to

upwards of £10,000 of which seven are on heritable security, and the remaining Three are in Bills, part at long dates, some at short - to meet these I have only about £1,000 per State (No2) consequently leaving a floating debt of £2,000 quite unprovided for. Of this however about £700 would not most likely press me. Thus it appears that even suffering all demands of mine tangible I would have a very large sum to raise to secure me from personal diligence. Previous however to entering on this part of the subject, I beg to call your attention to the annexed State (No3) of disbursements by which it appears that my heavy Debt has arisen nearly as follows.

Glasgow Debts	*£1,000*
Purchased improvements	*£5,375*
Involvements	*£2,040*

Having thus fully and candidly stated my actual situation and with its causes both remote and present I beg next to state what occurs to me as my best plan for extricating myself. The claims against me being so heavy, the interest payable annually must be nearly £500 and this is so enormous as to render every exertion to lessen it, not only prudent, but an act of absolute necessity. Having so long experienced the misery of renewing Bills, and borrowing money at heavy expense, I have made up my mind, to the propriety of selling Millbank. My reasons for this determination, in addition to these stated above are, that I concieve to be, by far the most valuable property I own, and as likely to bring its value. With respect to my other lands at Jaynefield, good judges have assured me that they consider it as ultimately the most valuable of the two, but in its present state, that to attempt selling it would only be throwing it away. Millbank I have reason to believe to be worth

£7,000 or thereby. Now this sum would so nearly clear me, as that all my debts would be paid up except a so small a proportion as my remaining Town rentals would pay the interest of. Now my dear Sir, being as before mentioned my natural Heir I beg to make you offer of the Lands of Millbank and I trust you will be induced to accept of them, both to keep them in the Family and as I trust they would be a purchase you would not have cause to regret.

You may probably say, what in this event do I intend doing myself, with my mother? My reply is my wish to build a Cottage at Janefield where everything is ready, and by so doing, I could live so much cheaper, as I hope, during my Mothers lifetime to clear off a great proportion of my remaining Debt, and at all events I would be infinitely more independent, than I can possibly be at Millbank.

Having thus fully explained myself, I shall anxiously wait for your decision when I trust you will comply with my wishes, or at least give me the benefit of your advice and judgement, as to what may be next best for me to adopt.

I remain My Dear Sir yrs very truly
Willm Mackintosh".

James replied –

"My dear Sir
I perused with deep concern your letter of yesterday. The state of your affairs was, till the receipt of that letter, altogether unknown to me and such a detail must, you may believe, have both grieved and surprised me. To extricate yourself from

embarrassments so very extensive will require on your part sacrifices which it is painful to contemplate. Property of every kind is now a good deal depreciated, and you are I fear a little sanguine in your calculations of relief. I should conceive Millbank considerably overrated at £7,000 and your debts amounting to upwards of £10,000 it is hard to say what additional sales may be necessary to extinguish them. In these circumstances I would suggest the propriety of not undertaking anything further in the building way at Janefield till you can ascertain whether there will be any & what reversion after payment of all incumbrances. The demands which now press upon you make your situation critical, and you should lose no time in taking competent advice as to the course which it will be proper for you to adopt. My purchasing Millbank at the price you have mentioned, or, indeed at any price, is out of the question. My engagements to my own family preclude it and nothing could induce me to put to hazard the future comfort of my wife, or the slender provision, which it has been in my power to make for my six daughters. I have besides numerous other burdens to provide for and have thus, on all occasions more to do than I have hitherto found to be prudent or convenient. I have thought it necessary to be thus explicit, however, disqualified by the state of my health and feelings for entering on so painful a subject. I write indeed with difficulty from the continued stiffness in my shoulder and can only add that I am My Dear Sir yours very truly".

Wood's map of Nairn shows a number of properties owned by William Mackintosh of Millbank and proposals for future development. Jaynefield, named after his wife, was to be part of a development along what is now called Waverley Road.

At the time when James declined William's offer he had six daughters with a seventh on the way. In Jane Austen's best seller, Pride and Prejudice, Mrs Bennett was concerned with but five. James was determined to set aside enough to provide for them. He was also concerned that his sister Helen and her husband Alex Grant should be able to look after his widowed mother and their young family.

As well as being involved with the Trusts of Margaret Mary Macdonald and Margaret Nona Mackintosh, he also held power of attorney in the UK for his wife's brother Guyon. The latter carried on trade between Madras and Padang in the Dutch East Indian island of Sumatra. He wrote to his sister Elizabeth that he had been somewhat scathing about William's lack of business sense.

> "He has taken offence but we still write to each other."

In December 1828 Mrs Colonel M died. This event should have eased William's financial woes, since he was due to receive a quarter of her funds which were held in trust by Donald Mackintosh. In fact it made matters worse.

Donald had been persuaded to lend trust funds to William in anticipation of his eventual share. It transpired that his share was less than the amount he had borrowed. Donald had invested some trust funds by way of bonds to friends with inadequate security. The Colonel's children were not happy with the way Donald had administered his widow's trust. William felt that his mother should have received a larger sum in interest which she was paying over to him while resident at Millbank. An interim payment from the trust was made to Elizabeth, Margaret Mary and Guyon but it was to be 1836 before a final settlement was reached. William's creditors also laid claim to some of the trust funds.

The children did however at this time receive an equal share of £1500 left to them by their mother's sister Mrs Peter Blaguire. James, having power of attorney in the UK, took charge of Guyon's share.

20. Deaths of Guyon and Aunt Mary

Guyon wrote regularly to his sisters. He told Elizabeth that he was getting fat and bald. In reply to James's letter informing him of his mother's death and the legacy from his Aunt Blaguire, he said in September 1829 that he was sorting the accounts of Kemp & Mackintosh after the former's recent death. He would come home but for his children, three boys and a girl. 2 boys were at school in Madras and the others with him in Padang. Captain Townsend lived nearby and had been a doctor and agent for him for many years.

The following month Mr Townsend wrote to James

> *"I have known Guyon for 14 years and have had his power of attorney here since his illness. All agree a return home would improve his health, but he is probably not up to the voyage. His objection is separation from his family and their mother who cares for him and for whom he has increased affection. He might agree to one trip to Europe for his health on Mr Roger's ship. He now considers India his home and requests me and Mr Storm to draw his funds to India. He has nominated you in his will as one of his executors."*

The will was changed, omitting James and specifying that Mr Townsend was to have nothing to do with his affairs.

For the meantime Guyon was most grateful for all that the Townsends had done for him and did not know how he could ever repay them for their kindness. It struck him that they would be very pleased to have a grand piano and asked Elizabeth to arrange for one to be sent from the UK. James organised the purchase of one in London and had it shipped out to Madras on one of Forbes & Co's vessels courtesy of the ever helpful William Bridgman.

Not long after this, Townsend reported that Guyon's physical health showed signs of improvement but his memory was defective. He used to repeat the same quotation over and over again.

John Storm in Calcutta, one of his oldest and most trusted friends, was concerned –

"Although Guyon wants his money in India, I strongly recommend his funds remain in England. Townsend thinks G's woman under a bad influence. T has legitimised the children so that they are heirs not legatees. This could have been done by marriage but he arranged adoption papers. I don't know if she is Christian or Pagan. The Resident takes an interest in him and his welfare. He's lately made a codicil to his will and increased his lady's legacy to include his house. I will try and get him to alter his will and make a settlement on his children."

James advised John Storm that all Guyon's funds were safely invested in the public funds. His legacy from Colonel M was in the British Linen Bank Inverness. He had written to Guyon seeking clear instructions from him.

Letters took at least four months to reach Padang from Nairn. Before he received a reply, John Storm broke the news of Guyon's death –

"Our dear Guyon breathed his last on 21 June 1831. Townsend advised Colonel Cadell who wrote to my brother. You have my deepest sympathies. Please break the news to Mrs Grant and William. I've advised Mrs Macdonald. Townsend intimates that my brother and self are executors in this country. Guyon left a letter requesting that the eldest boy be sent home. We've written to Madras for them all to be sent here (Calcutta) *and possibly all three should go."*

Margaret Macdonald sent James a copy of the letter she had received from John Storm. She would arrange for the reception of the poor boys into her family until James and William considered what should be done with them. Whilst awaiting to hear from Scotland the Storms had decided that they should send the three boys home.

John Storm wrote to James –

"Have sent the boys home in the Zenobia to the temporary charge of Mrs McD in Edinburgh, being unwilling to send them further north without your and William's permission. Sense you'll not approve. My brother and I are soon to leave this scene and the boys would then have noone to look after them. Think it essential to have them educated at home...."

James wrote to Margaret acknowledging her letter and unexpected situation –

"Although not what I recommended, their Guardians feel they should be educated here & perhaps best that the poor orphans be sent home. What do you think of them? Storm is silent about maintenance. Have consulted your brother and his wife who will take charge of the boys & place them at Nairn Academy. Couldn't expect more than £100 p.a. to cover their costs out of Guyon's funds. Please show Storm's letter to Donald Mackintosh for his information."

The fact, that the Storms in Calcutta were now acting as Guyon's executors rather than James as might have been expected, was likely to prolong any settlement of Colonel M's Trust.

James himself had recently become involved as sole executor of his Aunt Mary's estate. She had been the last surviving unmarried sister of Parson John. James neatly and methodically preserved evidence of his factorship for which he made no charge.

189

Aunt Mary rented a house in Nairn for £6 per annum from Baillie Ore. It was furnished by James's sister Helen's husband, Alex Grant of Dellachaple, to whom the furniture was returned. Apart from some minor items her estate consisted of a bond for £200 from the afore-mentioned Alex and one for £400 from the late Sir James Grant her clan chief. She left her estate equally between her three nieces, Helen, Elspet Cockburn and Elspet Clark. Her clothing was to go to Elspet Cockburn who had no father or brother to support her. She had made out her will herself.

Confirmation of the will was sworn to by James before William Mackintosh JP of Millbank and registered by Patrick Duff, Commissary Clerk Elgin. Duty of £17.0.6 at 3% was due to the Solicitor for legacy duty in Edinburgh. After funeral and other expenses each niece was due slightly over £180.

Helen received her husband's bill less expenses, while James gave each of the Elspets his own bill for £170 and the balance in cash. They would be paid interest on their bills half yearly. Although he did not recommend it, they could draw on their capital which would of course reduce their income. Aunt Mary wished to be buried with her beloved parents at Duthil.

Elspet Cockburn was content to draw her interest and preserve her capital. Elspet Clark was constantly badgered by her brother John for funds. Reluctantly James was obliged to let her draw on her bond to bail him out. She became afraid to keep approaching James and asked his wife to speak up for her and eventually her cousin Elspet Cockburn was used as an intermediary. Finally when she died all that was left of her "fortune" was £1.15s.6d.

The contrast between the two Elspets was mirrored in the circumstances of James and his wife's brother William. James's finances were sound, as befitted a shrewd business man. William frittered his fortune away borrowing unwisely for his grandiose schemes. He continued to ask his brother-in-law for help which on one occasion he rendered as a member of Nairn Burgh Council. William was due to pay them a significant sum by a certain date. James was able to persuade his colleagues to postpone the due date. The Provost, Sir William Gordon-Cumming, was James's friend and was instrumental in allowing William more leeway.

The composition of the Council has already been referred to. Sir William as Patron and Provost held considerable sway in Nairn just as Col Francis did in the Burgh of Forres. An example of the Colonel's influence has already been given in a letter he wrote to James about filling certain vacancies on the Council.

James continued to look out for the children of Alexander Carmichael who had been a fellow councillor in the early days. His widow had recently died leaving two unmarried daughters. Their brothers, Robert in Madras and Ludovick in Bengal provided funds for a trust which James, his friend Fraser Tytler and his neighbour in Nairn, Mr Grant of Seabank, administered for their support. They were tenants of Seafield Estates. James wrote to the Factor, Mr Fraser at Cullen concerning their rent and received the following reply.

"Dear Sir
I have corresponded with Colonel Grant on the subject of the joint application which you forwarded thro me from Mr Fraser Tytler, Mr Grant of Seabank and yourself on behalf of the Misses Carmichael; and he has really felt much at a loss what to say in answer to it; from his inclination to lend a favorable ear to a request from a quarter so respectable, on the one hand, and the delicacy of his own situation with reference to Lord Seafields affairs on the other, but on the whole he has made up his mind to drop a year's rent (about 20 guineas), if in your opinion that sum will be considered by the others concerned as sufficiently liberal on his part. Will you favor me with your individual sentiments about this preparatory to an ostensible answer being given to the application. Yrs etc."

JAG notes "Amount to be remitted acquiesced in, under the circumstances adverted to."

He regularly heard from both brothers with news of their part of India. A letter which Lt Robert Carmichael had sent James on 17 July 1825 arrived on 18 Jul 1826! It was addressed - Headquarters of the Army serving in Ava, Camp at Prome –

"My dear Sir
When I look at the date at which I am now addressing you, I blush to think I have not done myself this pleasure long ago. I have made several attempts to write and begun several letters, but being a very indifferent letter writer I have never been able to make one out to my own satisfaction, till now I am quite ashamed of my laziness and feel myself impelled to make another attempt to thank you for the very friendly part you have acted towards me. To your goodness and benevolence I am indebted for having placed me in the path which leads to honor and independence and I trust I shall prove myself not unworthy of the kind interest you have taken in me. Though my expressions of gratitude and thanks are made thus late, you will not on that account think they are the less sincere, but believe that I shall ever cherish the remembrance of the kind manner in which you took me by the hand.

My career in the service hitherto has been as fortunate as that of most young officers of the same standing as myself, and, the new organisation of the army gives us many advantages which we did not before possess, so that we are now animated by the hope of being Field Officers ere we become old men.
In consequence of each Battalion being formed into a Regiment, my old Corps, the 2nd Battalion of N. I. is now the 38th Regiment, to which I am still attached, and a Lieutenant, and am looking forward with

much pleasure to the period when I shall have climbed up the long list of Subalterns before me and obtained my Company.

I have been pressing my Mother and Brother to procure for me some good letters of introduction to persons in power in this part of the world. A strong recommendation to the notice of the Governor General, the Governor of Madras, to Colonel Morrison, the Commissary General or to Colonel Conway the Adjutant General of the Madras Army; to any of the Residents at any of the Native Courts, or indeed to any other person high in the service and holding an official situation might be most essentially serviceable to me, and, if it should at any time be in your power to obtain such a recommendation you will not I feel sure lose sight of your grateful protege R G Carmichael.

I have studied the Hindustani language in which I hope I have made some progress, so that in the event of my being lucky enough to be nominated to a staff appointment I trust I shall be able to fill (it) creditably to the service, my friends and myself.

I like the service much. It is the best in the world. I also like the Country and have been most fortunate in enjoyment of my health, never having been a day unwell since my arrival in India. I have not grown much since I left Scotland but am rather thinner, which is not against me, as fat folks dont thrive in this cool climate. I am a little changed in my appearance however in consequence of being well bronzed, or, as we term it here, having a little of the old Indian in my mug - the effects of leading a soldiers life under a burning tropical sun.

194

Our Regiment has been in this Country about three months and with the Head Quarters about six weeks. Since our arrival there has nothing in the way of fighting taken place. We are now tolerably comfortable in our Monsoon Quarters where we must remain until the beginning of November when the rains will have broken less. We then march for Ummerapoora the Capital of the Empire. We expect to meet with little or no resistance on the road as the Burmese are greatly disheartened since the death of their General Bundoolah and the war must very soon be brought to a conclusion. General Morrison with the Bengal Division has taken Arracan and marches at the same time as us for the capital. We are to form a junction about 150 miles from this and the two armies will drive everything before them. This is a delightful climate and the troops are very healthy.

Pray remember me most kindly to Mrs Grant and all your young people. I hope they are all quite well and you yourself in the enjoyment of good health. John will now be becoming quite a young man. Ask him if he recollects me and say I never forget him.

Perhaps you will be good enough to make offer of my kind remembrances to my friends at Seabank and to worthy Mrs Carmichael and Miss Mary Grant. Tell them all that I think of them though far away. Yrs etc Address 38th Regiment Madras N I, c/o Messrs Arbuthnot & Co."

21. Death of Uncle George & JAG's mother

With Walker now on St Helena, James had received less information and comment on events in what had been their part of India. He gleaned a certain amount about happenings from the "Asiatic Journal" but little about the personalities involved. He still kept in touch with Francis Warden who wrote from Bombay –

"My dear friend.
Do you recollect such a place as Ambolee? I think not. For whilst I, as an assistant in the office, stole away to Salsette on a Saturday and Sunday, James Augustus was not at Church, but extracting from old musty records information for a long Minute on Surat or Baroda affairs, or about the Malwa or Singanian piracies. We have been here for a fortnight away from the dust of Bombay, stay till the 22d, and on the 27th start for the Caves of Elma.

I have two letters from you on my file of the 6 of Dec and 25 of Jan last. In the first you wrote of your brother George's boys.

Your other letter was introductory of Burnett. He was housed before he came to me - that attention I could not therefore extend to him as I am cordially disposed to do to all your recommendations. He soon passed in the Hindustani and is now in this same Island of Salsette, in which Collectorship he is an assistant. He appears to be of more sturdy constitution than his Cousins & promises to turn out as well - may he be destined to enjoy a longer life.

You write a much better hand than the scratches you have left in the office, some of which passed under my notice about a month ago as I was trawling the despatches to the Court from 1800 to 1803 in preparing my compilation of the History of Bombay, in which I was employing myself. You may fairly repay the compliment!

Do you use spectacles? I have not yet become such a spectacle but all around me either stretch out a paper at arms length or that failing put on their spectacles to read the clearest writing. Not so James Wilson who has the command to his great joy of the Residency division & is as hearty as when he paid his advances to Nancy Whitcombe and Fanny Crozier. I do not believe there is another of your old friends in Bombay - yes there are. M... and Gregory. The former in Bellasis place and the latter in the Native Section which I established. There is Matthews too, who you may recollect drawing Bell & Smith. He is now the Head Clerk in one of three divisions with which the duties have been split with a salary of 500Rs a month, what I received as Deputy Secretary. All these office details will give you more pleasure than official news. These have now expanded into such a space that I should only be bewildering you were I to enter into my exhibition of our present state. You must therefore have patience till my History is out, and if you know Jeffery, pray bespeak a merciful review. By the bie why should you not undertake that duty. I should then have "justice" done me.

Adieu my dear friend yours affectionately

F Warden".

Since his retirement more than twenty years ago from the HEIC, James had been able by 1832 to advance the careers of several relations and friends, such as Burnett of Elrick's sons and nephew, by introductions to persons with whom he had served.

James on one occasion received a letter from the son of a former employee Willibar Ballagee to whom he replied –

"I received in May 1827 your letter of the 7th Dec 1826 and this day, that of the 2d April last. Of the first I have too long omitted to acknowledge the receipt; but I did not overlook the object of it. Being myself a good distance from London, I wrote to Mr Morris formerly Secretary at Bombay, and now one of the East India Directors, to attend to your wishes, and you will see by his answer, which is now enclosed, that he promised his best exertions to promote the success of your application. What has since been done, I have not heard, but both on your own, and your late worthy fathers account, I hope your services will be properly rewarded.
I remain Your wellwisher
J A Grant."

Chas Forbes was now a Baronet. He had acquired the parliamentary seat of Beverley. He kept in regular contact with James, always asking after his wife Elizabeth, who as the young bride of his friend and protege had so impressed him. His sister was married to Major Dan Mitchell who had grown up with the Grants and their Forbes cousins at

Inverernan in Strathdon. He was staying there when Major Alex Forbes, the eldest of James's Forbes cousins, died.

He sent James a copy of a letter which he had sent to Sir Charles informing him of the event. Alex's two brothers John and George had died in India.

George had been named after his uncle George Grant, one of the brothers of James's mother. Uncle George had a daughter Eliza, Mrs du Bois, with whom James used to correspond after the death of her mother Aunt Foster. She was to write of the death of her father –

"My dear & valued Cousin
How inadequate are words to express the feelings of the soul, when the heart is almost bursting with the conflicting emotions of love, veneration and grief - mine has indeed been thus painfully excited since yesterday week, when I accidentally and most unexpectedly heard that my revered and beloved Father was very ill at Paris, to which place he had gone from the Netherlands a few weeks ago, & that a friend and physician had written an account of his illness to Mrs Thelluson's son, which caused them so much alarm that dearest Susan (who had only returned home 3 weeks from hence having been staying with us to nurse and comfort me after my painful attack of rheumatic fever in the Autumn) with Jane, immediately started for Paris, and thank God arrived in time to afford that only consolation & comfort to our beloved and only parent, his painful and alarming illness could admit of. You know the good and estimable qualities of my lamented and

beloved Father, and will I am sure enter into my feelings on this most distressing occasion. We received a more favourable account Thursday and Friday, which made me cling to hope that his naturally fine & strong constitution would be enabled to resist this attack, and that we might yet have been blessed with him for years & and that his ultimate recovery might be hoped for. I was therefore unwilling to write and alarm you and his other dear relations in the North - but alas! it would now perhaps have been better had I done so, as I greatly fear you will have seen this melancholy event in the papers a day before this can reach you. I think the publishers have been very hasty as they must have been told to insert next week - saying ultimo - when this heartrending loss occurred on Wednesday the 21st Inst at 8 oclock in the morning. I have not yet received all the particulars of this mournful loss as poor Susan was so deeply affected to be enabled to write them to me in the few lines I only received from her last, nor can I describe to you how deeply I deplore not having been able to soothe & endeavour also to comfort the departing moments of our lamented & suffering parent. His attack was a violent crysepitas in his legs. The moment Susan arrived she wrote to the first friend and English physician to meet the gentleman who had been previously attending him, and had the gratification to hear that everything had been done that was right, & that our beloved Father could not have had better advice than the first attendant had given him. Alas! the ease our poor father felt soon after my sister arrived and which had given them and us hope was the fatal symptom of approaching loss & as doubtless the mortification had taken place. They got to Paris on Saturday the 17th inst & sunday dear Susan said to him she thought he looked better than on the *preceding day. He replied "that is because you are come to nurse me" - Sweet words to poor Susan as she observes - he was delighted to see them. His sons most unfortunately were not one of them able to be there & are in various places far distant. The blow is thus doubly felt. My dearest Father so anxiously enquired after my health of Susan, ill as he was & said how glad he was to hear of its amendment. My heart is so afflicted I cannot write any more.*

Give my affectionate love to dear "Mrs JAG" & all your young ones. Thank my dear Cousin for her kind letter and accept yourself the affectionate regard of your afflicted unhappy Cousin Eliza Mary DuBois.

Will you my dear Cousin be kind enough to communicate this melancholy intelligence to your Mother, Doctor & Mrs Forbes & Mrs Major Forbes and you will confer as an obligation - say I have requested you to do so. God bless you."

Doctor Forbes was the husband of Major Forbes's sister Mary.

James was very concerned for his mother. Since Parson John's death in 1820 she had made her home at Garmouth with her only daughter Helen, Mrs Alex Grant. Initially she visited Viewfield regularly to see her seven granddaughters. Latterly, when she found travelling difficult, the Viewfields would visit her at Garmouth where Alex with James's help had built a house on land given him by his friend and employer Grant of Rothiemurchus.

Alex had died on 19 June 1829. Unbeknown to his widow he was in some financial difficulty. James was in touch with Helen's lawyer in Elgin, Mr Bain, and wrote to him –

"My dear Sir
Since I had the pleasure of seeing you the affairs of my late brother-in-law have occupied my thoughts a good deal; and I continue to feel very anxious on the subject.

The magnitude and variety of his engagements and responsibility would seem to proscribe the necessity of great caution. Under this impression I addressed to you this morning the enclosed letter, and it may be proper to add, in explanation, that I was induced to do so, partly from finding by a letter from our deceased friend, dated in 1816 (the year in which he left Glasgow) that he had just then compounded with his creditors, and was allowed two years from that time to pay his instalments. Now it occurs to me as possible, that the demand from Glasgow, for which an amount was rendered in 1824 might have been a remnant of the debts under that composition, and hence the necessity of seeing that all is clear before my sister comes under any engagement to pay all private debts. Again as to his management under the Assignees (of Rothiemurchus), we know that one of them Mr James Grant W.S. has become insolvent, and that another Mr Cowper has been living in doubtful credit, and might give trouble were an opening left. In these circumstances it is material to see, that the late Mr Grant's accounts while acting under, and responsible to them, have been regularly passed, and, so, also, in respect to his Agency under Mr Borthwick; and, lastly, as to his personal obligations to Rothiemurchus's creditors, you will, I am sure, agree with me, that Mrs Grant would not be warranted in conveying to them the heritable property and shipping without the certainty of a final discharge.

From the first I dreaded the consequences to Mr Grant's family of his heavy engagements for Rothiemurchus; and having already lost £1500 by his failure in Glasgow, besides £1000 given to my sister on her marriage, it is impossible for me without losing sight of my obligations to my own numerous fireside, to lend my name again, till relieved from all apprehension of risk. My funds are in fact so destined, that I could not honestly expose them to hazard, and more I need not say to engage your good offices to keep us all safe. I have details I give you in confidence, and I know they will be confined to your own breast, because the disclosure of them would be painful to my sister; but if you think it will do any good to send a copy of the accompanying letter to Mr Cook, you may do so; and wishing you many happy returns of the season, I always am my dear Sir most truly yours etc

PS Pray have you heard whether Mr Cook has got me ranked on the Trust estate of Rothiemurchus for the £200 Bill I enclosed to you on the 4th of July last, and which you forwarded to him for that purpose."

James cared for his relations and had relieved many of them in their financial distress. He had become a sound businessman aware of the necessity to protect his own and his sister's positions.

It was important that Helen should be given all possible help as their mother was becoming increasingly frail and reliant upon her.

She died peacefully on 21st July 1832.

In a letter to Miss Elspet Clark of the 27th July, concerning her inheritance from her Aunt Miss Mary Grant, James informed her that he had returned the previous night from Garmouth after paying the last duties to the remains of his lamented mother.

Helen and James were their parents only surviving children. Nine years later they decided to erect a memorial in Duthil churchyard to all the Grants of Milton at the grave where Parson John had been laid to rest.

For now it was the end of an era. James had conscientiously kept the 5th Commandment:

"Honour thy father and thy mother that the days of thy life may be long in the land which the Lord Thy God giveth thee".

Fittingly, although already fifty five, he was destined in the course of another thirty six eventful years to live to be ninety one.

Looking back –

He had exchanged a life as a Judge and senior member of the HEIC in India for that of a Councillor and Provost of Forres. The long years of war with Republican France had ended with Wellington's defeat of Napoleon at Waterloo. He had afforded his parents comfort by his achievements and especially in his choice of a wife.

Sadly he had lost his only son, but Elizabeth had given him seven beautiful daughters of whom he was very fond. His wider family had produced many nieces and nephews, some of them born to Indian women and experiencing contrasting fortunes.

Although he had kept in touch with many friends from his Bombay days, hardly any of them now remained there. Help had been given to relations and friends, not least to the Storm brothers by his twelve hundred mile round trip to London that Christmas to vote in person for their benefactor.

It had been an age of patronage, with his friend Colonel Francis often being involved. Now, in 1832, all that seemed likely to change with the introduction of Bills for electoral and other reforms. He could look forward to a very different life. It is described in a sequel to this book entitled "Viewfield".

Index

A

COCKBURN, John Senior, 25, 26, 27, 46
CROWE, Judge, 35, 125
Cullen, 45, 86, 139, 150, 192
Culloden, 47, 51, 52
CUMMING, George M.P., 174

D

DIGGLE, 31, 57
DU BOIS, See GRANT Cousin Eliza
DUNCAN, Jonathan, 11, 12, 13, 15, 20, 54, 56, 69, 70, 122
Duthil, 25, 39, 143, 190, 204

F

FORBES, Aunt Betty, 10, 22, 111, 114
FORBES, Charles, 15, 54, 67, 69, 70, 71, 72, 91, 92, 93, 103, 122, 123,
    124, 125, 126, 198, 199
FORBES, Cousin Alexander, 10, 114, 199
FORBES, Cousin George, 10, 22, 199
FORBES, Cousin John, 10, 19, 22, 199
FORBES, Cousin Mary, 10, 22, 201
FORBES, John (Head of Forbes & Co), 69, 92, 93, 125
FORBES, Michie, 93, 152, 153
FORBES, Uncle Alexander, 10
Forres, 9, 27, 49, 60, 63, 75, 86, 87, 88, 115, 116, 117, 138, 139, 140, 147,
    149, 172, 173, 174, 176, 191, 205
FOSTER, Aunt, 10, 13, 66, 96, 110, 113, 114, 115, 118, 127, 154, 156, 169,
    170, 171, 199
FOSTER, Mrs. *See* GRANT, Jane (nee DALTON)

G

GALLOWAY, Jane, Mrs William Mackintosh Millbank 63, 67, 68, 165
Garmouth, 102, 114, 147, 149, 150, 158, 169, 201, 204
GORDON, John (Banker), 75,
GORDON-CUMMING, Sir William, 175, 191
GRANT, Alex, Dellachapel, 13, 26, 29, 46, 98, 99, 100, 101, 102, 104,
    105, 106, 107, 111, 113, 114, 143, 149, 157, 158, 184, 190, 201, 202
GRANT, Aunt Anne See COCKBURN Aunt Anne
GRANT, Aunt Eliza (Parson John's sister), 25, 26, 29, 46
GRANT, Aunt Elizabeth. *See* FORBES, Aunt Betty
GRANT, Aunt Janet, 25, 26, 46, 49
GRANT, Aunt Mary, 25, 26, 28, 46, 108, 189, 190, 204
GRANT, Brother George, 10, 13, 14, 19, 26, 46, 96, 111, 131, 133, 135,
    136, 150, 151, 152, 154, 155, 157, 160, 162

GRANT, Brother Peter, 10, 13, 14, 26, 46
GRANT, Brother Sweton, 10, 13, 26, 46, 53
GRANT, Charles (Lord Glenelg), 33
GRANT, Christian, 10, 13, 17, 26, 40, 41, 42, 46, 160, 196, 199, 204
GRANT, Colonel the Hon Francis, 9, 36, 39, 41, 42, 44, 45, 76, 86, 88, 100, 117, 139, 140, 148, 150, 157, 172, 176, 191, 192, 205
GRANT, Cousin Elizabeth, Mrs Du Bois, 199, 201
GRANT, Cousin Foster, 40, 41, 42, 96, 155
GRANT, Cousin Jane, 169, 170, 199
GRANT, Cousin Mary, 155, 156, 157
GRANT, Cousin Susan,110, 199
GRANT, Daughter Augusta, 68, 127, 142
GRANT, Daughter Christina, 68, 121, 142
GRANT, Daughter Eliza, 68, 90, 108, 142
GRANT, Daughter Helen, 68, 166
GRANT, Daughter Jamesina, 68, 172, 178
GRANT, Daughter Margaret Mary, 68, 166
GRANT, Daughter Mary Foster, 68, 171
GRANT, Great Uncle Patrick, 46, 47, 49
GRANT, James Augustus (Nephew), 29
GRANT, James Ballintomb, 46, 49
GRANT, James Thomas, 38
GRANT, Jane (nee DALTON), 41, 42, 96, 111, 112, 169
GRANT, Johnnie, 68, 76, 80, 96, 141, 172, 177, 178, 180
GRANT, Lady Francis, 41, 58
GRANT, Lewis, 37, 38, 39, 42, 43, 44
GRANT, Marjory Ballintomb, 111, 114, 147, 157
GRANT, Rev Alexander, 49, 50, 53, 76
GRANT, Rev James ('Young Jamie'), 53
GRANT, Rev John (Parson John), 10, 13, 14, 17, 19, 20, 22, 23, 24, 25, 26, 29, 37, 40, 42, 46, 47, 48, 50, 65, 66, 73, 76, 80, 100, 111, 114, 136, 141, 142, 143, 144, 145, 147, 149, 150, 151, 154, 170, 189, 201, 204
GRANT, Sir James, 37, 38, 39, 41, 42, 43, 44, 48, 190
GRANT, Sister Helen, 10, 13, 26, 29, 46, 98, 99, 100, 107, 108, 111, 113, 114, 143, 147, 153, 184, 190, 201, 202, 204
GRANT, Sweton (Grandfather), 46, 48, 49
GRANT, Uncle George, 10, 13, 39, 41, 42, 96, 110, 196, 199
GRANT, Uncle James Augustus (Uncle JAG), 10, 11, 13, 20, 21, 22, 38, 66
GRANT, Uncle Patrick, 23, 26, 46, 48
GRANT, William, Dellachapel, 25, 26, 46, 48
GRANT, William, Seabank, 45, 62, 78, 87, 192
Gujerat, 12, 14, 15, 31, 35, 57, 150
GUYON, Elizabeth Claudia. *See* MACKINTOSH, Mrs Col.

MONEY, William, 70, 72, 123, 124, 125, 126, 127, 128, 151
MORRIS, John, 122, 198

N

NAPOLEON, 17, 18, 19, 27, 57, 74, 75, 80, 81, 82, 96, 97, 99, 104, 105, 114, 168, 205
NICOLLS, General, 28, 102, 103, 104

P

PALMERSTON, Lord, 148
PERCEVAL, Spencer, P.M., 73, 74
PHILIPPS, Dr Benjamin, 161
PHILIPS, James, 149, 175

R

RICKARDS, Robert, 32, 33, 36, 56, 91, 92, 95, 123
ROSE, Captain (Executor of GRANT, George), 152, 153, 160, 161, 162
ROSE, Captain James, 119, 176
ROSE, Hugh of Kilravock, 141
Rothiemurchus, 89
ROTHIEMURCHUS, J.P.GRANT of, 102, 113, 143, 158, 159, 201, 202, 203

S

Seabank, 45, 62, 78, 87, 192, 195
SHANK, Henry, 54, 56, 83, 131, 139, 152, 154, 168
SIDMOUTH, Lord, 140
SMITH, John, 124
St Helena, 97, 167, 168, 196
STEADMAN, William, 35, 36
STORM, John, 121, 129, 130, 164, 186, 187, 188, 189, 205
STORM, William, 121, 122, 127, 128, 129, 130, 164, 188, 189, 205
STUART, General, 15
Surat, 35, 132, 196

T

THELLUSON, Charles, 156
THELLUSON, Mrs Mary. *See* GRANT, Cousin Mary
THRIEPLAND, 34, 35, 70, 71
TOWNSEND, 186, 187, 188

W

WALKER, Alexander, 15, 16, 29, 30, 32, 33, 34, 35, 57, 58, 59, 65, 70, 82, 97, 121, 144, 152, 153, 166, 167, 168, 196
WALLACE, Dr, 57
WARDEN, Francis (Frank), 28, 31, 55, 72, 82, 83, 131, 151, 152, 153, 154, 161, 162, 196, 197
Waterloo, 93, 98, 205
WELLESLEY, General Arthur. *See* WELLINGTON, Duke of
WELLESLEY, Marquis, 11, 12, 18, 27, 72
WELLINGTON, Duke of, 17, 18, 72, 73, 74, 75, 80, 81, 97, 115, 172, 173, 205
WILLIAMS, 154, 161, 162
WILLIAMSON, Captain, 45, 59, 64, 65